NORTH KOREA

WHAT EVERYONE NEEDS TO KNOW®

NORTH KOREA

WHAT EVERYONE NEEDS TO KNOW®

PATRICK McEACHERN

OXFORD
UNIVERSITY PRESS

Oxford University Press is a department of the University of Oxford. It furthers the University's objective of excellence in research, scholarship, and education by publishing worldwide. Oxford is a registered trade mark of Oxford University Press in the UK and certain other countries.

"What Everyone Needs to Know" is a registered trademark of Oxford University Press.

Published in the United States of America by Oxford University Press 198 Madison Avenue, New York, NY 10016, United States of America.

CIP data is on file at the Library of Congress
ISBN 978-0-19-093798-0 (pbk.)
ISBN 978-0-19-093799-7 (hbk.)

1 3 5 7 9 8 6 4 2

Paperback printed by Sheridan Books, Inc., United States of America
Hardback printed by Bridgeport National Bindery, Inc., United States of America

For Jaclyn and Timmy

CONTENTS

3 Post–Cold War   56

4 Nuclear Weapons and US–North Korea Relations   71

9 The Economy   151

10 Korean Society: North and South   162

11 North Korean Human Rights   185

ACKNOWLEDGMENTS

The production of any book inevitably involves many more people than the author named on the cover, and this volume is no different. I had the good fortune of writing *What Everyone Needs to Know about North Korea* while on a leave of absence from the State Department and in residence at the Wilson Center as a Council on Foreign Relations (CFR) International Affairs Fellow, from September 2017 to August 2018. Consequently, there are many people to recognize and thank.

The Council on Foreign Relations funded my fellowship year and allowed me the time and space to take a break from the operational demands of foreign policy, learn the roles of a public intellectual, and write this book. In New York, I appreciate the hard work of CFR Director of Fellowship Affairs Janine Hill and Deputy Director Victoria Harlan that made this possible for me. In Washington, my thanks to CFR Director of the Program on U.S.-Korea Policy Scott Snyder, who graciously integrated me into many of the roundtables and symposia at the council. Scott is a true intellectual from whom I learn much every time I get to hear him speak or attend one of his thoughtful events, and those sessions helped inform this book. Thanks also to CFR's Pattie Kim, who is clearly a rising star in foreign policy analysis in Northeast Asia.

My intellectual home for my fellowship year was the Wilson Center in Washington, DC, and it is hard to imagine a

more collaborative research environment. A special thank you
to the Wilson Center's Senior Vice President and Director of
International Security Studies Rob Litwak, who first welcomed
me into the Wilson family, provided specific writing and conference opportunities, and offered countless truly helpful
comments. His selfless leadership and perceptive insights
drive the foreign policy analysis and analysts at Wilson to
probe deeper and maximize policy impact, including this book
and this author.

At Wilson, I also learned more than I can adequately express
from Korea Program Director Jean Lee. Jean is the driving force
behind the rapid expansion of the Korea program, yet always
found time to assist all of us in our research and public engagement strategies alike. Asia Program Director Abe Denmark,
Deputy Director Michael Kugelman, Senior Northeast Asia
Associate Shihoto Goto, and Public Policy Fellows Soojin Park,
Kevin Gray, and Taekyoon Kim all contributed to this book in
countless conversations throughout the course of the year and
beyond.

The intellectual curiosity of scholars outside the Asia program at Wilson and generous, constructive feedback helped
me consider more angles and speak to a broader audience.
There are too many scholars to recognize individually, so allow
me a collective thank you. Finally, the Wilson Center librarians
are second to none. A small, three-person team led by Janet
Spikes, the Wilson Center librarians are the institution's secret weapon. I am convinced there is no resource they could
not find, and their proactive effort to identify additional
source material for this and so many other projects is simply a
researcher's dream.

Thank you to my many hard-working colleagues at the
State Department. I appreciate the institution allowing me to
take a year off and all those who read through my drafts in
the prepublication review process. As I always promised that
I would note, let me assure the reader that the views expressed

here do not necessarily reflect those of the US government or Department of State.

At Oxford University Press, it was my great fortune to get to meet and work with Vice President and Executive Editor Nancy Toff. I have had the good luck of working with several top-notch book editors over the years, but Nancy is in a league by herself. Her professionalism, timeliness, superb communication, and keen judgment are just some of the attributes that make it such a joy to work with her. Thank you also to Assistant Editor Elizabeth Vaziri and two thoughtful anonymous reviewers who contributed substantially to this book.

Last but not least, my thanks go to my loveliest of past coauthors and wife, Jaclyn, and our son, Timothy. Your love, support, and critique had a truly positive mark on this work and on me more generally. All of those mentioned above, and I am sure others I have failed to mention, had a profound impact on me and this book. Nevertheless, all remaining errors are mine alone—unless someone else wants to claim them.

NORTH KOREA

WHAT EVERYONE NEEDS TO KNOW®

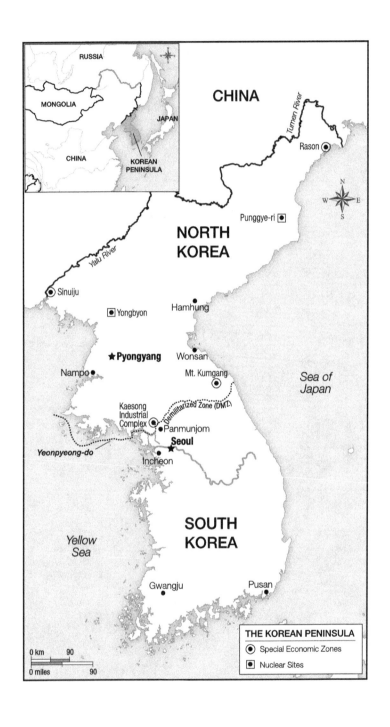

RUSSIA

MONGOLIA

JAPAN

CHINA

KOREAN
PENINSULA

CHINA

Tumen River

Rason

Punggye-ri

NORTH
KOREA

N
W   E
S

Yalu River

Sinuiju

Yongbyon   Hamhung

Pyongyang   Wonsan

Nampo   Mt. Kumgang   Sea of
Japan

Kaesong
Industrial   Demilitarized Zone (DMZ)
Complex   Panmunjom

Seoul

Yeonpyeong-do

Incheon

SOUTH
KOREA

Yellow
Sea

Gwangju   Pusan

THE KOREAN PENINSULA

◉ Special Economic Zones

▣ Nuclear Sites

0 km   90

0 miles   90

INTRODUCTION

On November 28, 2017, North Korean leader Kim Jong Un professed his nuclear deterrent "complete." After a year of trading colorful barbs with the American president that dangerously raised the chances of miscalculation and war on the peninsula, as well as significant achievements in North Korea's decades-long nuclear and missile development programs, Kim declared his mission accomplished. Although Kim's pronouncement appears to have been premature, North Korea is on the verge of being able to strike the United States with nuclear weapons. South Korea, Japan, and American troops stationed in both countries have long been in North Korea's crosshairs, but the United States' most important allies in Asia have based their national security on a calculation that the United States would defend them if they were attacked. North Korea's gaining the ability to strike the continental United States with nuclear weapons erodes their confidence that an American president would jeopardize Seattle to help Seoul when the chips are down. North Korea's nuclear advances rattle the basic foundations of security in one of the most militarized, populous, and prosperous corners of the globe.

Despite the pessimistic outlook in 2017, diplomacy took a sudden turn in 2018, when North Korean Chairman Kim Jong Un offered to talk to his South Korean and American counterparts. Kim Jong Un and US President Donald Trump had been dropping provocative threats of military attacks on each other as South Korean President Moon Jae-in was welcoming the North Korean Olympic team and senior officials to the Winter Olympics that South Korea hosted in February 2018. In just four months after the world had witnessed President Moon welcome the North Koreans to the South Korean Winter Olympics, Moon not only orchestrated another inter-Korean summit in April but also brokered the first ever US–North Korea summit, to take place in June. The diplomatic whiplash appropriately captured international headlines as journalists rushed to document the rapid changes, but short articles or TV coverage rarely offered substantial opportunity to provide the richer background. The North Korean about-face is naturally perplexing on the surface, as are many of the issues surrounding the seemingly mysterious country. Examining some of the deeper context helps to shed some light on the regime's behavior.

North Korea: What Everyone Needs to Know seeks to demystify North Korea on these contemporary questions and many others. North Korea's foreign policy and the nuclear issue dominate the news coverage of the country, but a deeper dive is needed to explain why the country acts the way it does. This book makes no excuses for the Kim family's political choices, but it attempts to show the context, rationale, and trade-offs of its decisions. North Korea's history, relations with its neighbors and the United States, the peculiarities of its political leadership, and the social and economic context help set the stage for understanding today's opportunities and challenges with respect to this country.

As with most issues in international affairs, the best place to begin is with the history.

Koreans are an ancient people, but North Korea and South Korea established themselves as separate states only in 1948. Following a bitterly opposed Japanese occupation and colonization of Korea (1910–1945) that ended abruptly with Japan's defeat in World War II, the American and Soviet superpowers divided the Korean Peninsula into two zones of influence. Two competing Korean regimes developed and each government claimed to be the rightful ruler of the entire Korean Peninsula. North Korea initially had the upper hand in both military and economic areas and sought to eliminate its rival early, in the 1950–1953 Korean War. North Korea surely would have succeeded in its war effort within months if not weeks had it not been for the United States' military intervention. For North Korea, the Americans would from that point forward be considered the despised impediment to the unification of their nation under Pyongyang's leadership. North Korea then, as now, considered the United States, not South Korea, its primary enemy and security threat.

Nevertheless, the two Korean governments were clearly Cold War rivals. Seoul and Pyongyang both sought international legitimacy to represent the Korean people, and today's contrast between a democratic and prosperous South Korea versus an authoritarian and poor North Korea was not present. North Korea enjoyed better economic growth than South Korea during the first half of the Cold War, and South Korea's own authoritarian government presented a contrast between a left-wing dictatorship in the North and a right-wing one in the South. North Korea worried about the American threat to its security, but it compared itself to South Korea and wanted to come out on top.

The end of the Cold War brought stunning changes and even revolution to many of the Soviet satellite states, and it had a lasting impact on the Korean Peninsula. With the Soviet demise, North Korea lost its primary security and economic patron; the country descended into crisis and famine in the 1990s as its rival in the South was demonstrating its clear economic superiority and consolidating its newfound democracy. North Korea's traditional allies in Moscow and Beijing established diplomatic relations with Seoul, which Pyongyang saw as nothing short of betrayal, and South Korea's growing economic fortunes translated into political clout in foreign affairs. However, the

Kim regime did not collapse, as some had predicted, in part, because it differed from other Soviet satellite states and had for decades built a more independent country. Nevertheless, the political and security relationships on and around the Korean Peninsula changed rapidly after the end of the Cold War, and the changes did not favor North Korea. This period brought the nuclear issue to the fore. Long in the background, North Korea's nuclear ambitions reached an acute crisis in the 1990s when it faced increasingly challenging internal and external environments. North Korea used brinkmanship and diplomacy as the countries around North Korea called on it to denuclearize. The United States and North Korea produced a bilateral nuclear accord, called the 1994 Agreed Framework, which, after several years of shaky implementation, ultimately fell apart. The bilateral nuclear negotiating framework gave way in 2003 to a multilateral one involving the two Koreas, the United States, China, Japan, and Russia. The Six Party Talks tackled the same problems with many of the same carrots and sticks used in the US–North Korea effort, and the Six Party Talks, like the Agreed Framework before it, delayed and degraded North Korea's nuclear program but did not end it. This nuclear negotiating history would help inform the analysis and advocacy surrounding the current round of nuclear diplomacy with Pyongyang.

While relations between regional powers are woven into the fabric of the nuclear diplomacy, many other issues intersect in Northeast Asia. China is the largest trading partner for both North Korea and South Korea, but its economic relationship with each is fundamentally different. China trades with South Korea on commercial terms for profit, while it reluctantly continues concessionary terms of trade and aid for North Korea for political ends, including preserving stability on its border.

Japan colonized the entire Korean Peninsula from 1910 to 1945, and the governments in Seoul and Pyongyang share a disdain for that experience. Nevertheless, the intervening seven decades have raised other separate issues with Japan for each Korean government. For example, Japan's urging North Korea to return the Japanese citizens it abducted in the late 1970s and early 1980s continues to animate that bilateral relationship. The United States and South Korea are military allies facing a shared threat from North Korea, yet issues of Korean identity, human rights, and trade can at times complicate the alliance. The complex web of issues among the regional powers helps to provide recent background on stories in the news and to explain the complex calculations being made in each capital.

Although states may have interests, leaders make decisions. Consequently, no assessment of North Korea is complete without providing background on the Kim dynasty—and the leaders they face across the DMZ in Seoul. The three Kims in North Korea, who have ruled the country since its founding—Kim Il Sung, Kim Jong Il, and Kim Jong Un—have distinct personalities, ruling styles, and even objectives. In South Korea, the differences between its leaders are even more stark; South Korean conservatives and progressives disagree strongly on the proper approach to North Korea policy.

Political leaders and systems do not operate without reference to the people they seek to rule. Social and economic issues in North Korea and South Korea may be in the background in discussions of matters of high politics, but they have a profound effect on the long-term trajectory of the Korean Peninsula. Beyond the contrast between the South Korean economic success and North Korean economic failure, what more can we say about these two systems? What are the everyday lives of Koreans in these two countries like? Put differently, if North Koreans and South Koreans are one people, do individuals in each country live in basically similar or fundamentally different ways? In extreme form, how does the North Korean regime treat its citizens and deal with their basic human rights?

After a review of North Korea's history, nuclear development, political leadership and the regional dynamics and social and economic matters in the two Koreas, we will get an opportunity to leverage this understanding of North Korea's past and present to hazard a guess about its future. Looking ahead is always more difficult than looking back, but all forward-looking assessments are not equal. Informed speculation is inherently better than uninformed speculation, but it means narrowing the scope of uncertainty without making a definitive pronouncement on North Korea's years ahead. Reasonable people will disagree. This book endeavors to arm the reader with an understanding of the basic contours that inform the contemporary policy debates surrounding North Korea. It invites the reader to critically engage the questions facing policymakers and concerned citizens, in many countries, and to come up with better alternatives to the important and challenging issues that reverberate well beyond North Korea's borders.

1

ORIGINS AND
THE KOREAN WAR

What is Korea's "5,000 years of history"?

Koreans occasionally refer to their people's "5,000 years of history," a description that reflects a well-placed pride in the long and continuous succession of their nation despite having larger nations around them that assimilated others. Korea has not been a singular political unit for five thousand years, and it was wiped off the map completely as late as the first half of the twentieth century, when Japan annexed the country. Its borders and political divisions have changed, but the Korean people have been around for a long time and have distinguished themselves from those who would become the Chinese and the Japanese, in particular.

As in much of the world, the earliest archeological evidence of the presence of people in Korea dates back to the Paleolithic Age, when people lived in caves and eked out a basic existence. Between 6000 and 5000 BCE, people in Korea started developing tools and pottery. The designs became increasingly sophisticated and, around 2000 BCE, showed a marked cultural influence from neighboring China. The inhabitants of the Korean Peninsula started to merge as they shifted from hunting and gathering to agriculture, specifically cultivating rice. These communities became the basis of the Korean race and society.

The rise of walled towns gave way to a variety of kingdoms across the peninsula as these societies developed spirituality, coins, law, culture, and hereditary political succession. These communities fought with the Chinese, which became the most important influence on cultural development and foreign affairs. Around the first century CE, the ancient kingdoms of Goguryeo, Baekje, and Silla emerged in what became known as the Three Kingdoms period. Goguryeo was the largest geographically, taking up the northern part of the Korean Peninsula and extending into modern-day China and Russia. Baekje occupied the southwest corner of the peninsula, and Silla, the southeast corner. The three kingdoms allied and fought with one another—and the Chinese—for hundreds of years.

In the late seventh century, the southeastern kingdom of Silla unified the Korean people for the first time under one political organization in the Unified Silla dynasty. Unified Silla's authoritarian practices gave way to rebellion and a long decline. Local power brokers, however, retained significant influence in practice because the central government failed to maintain deep control over the country. Unified Silla fell in the early tenth century, and was replaced by the Goryeo dynasty, from which the modern name "Korea" comes.

The Goryeo dynasty lasted for almost half a millennium, but a generation of fighting with the Mongols and Chinese weakened the regime, and Goryeo fell to another Korean dynasty, Joseon. The Joseon dynasty ruled Korea from 1392 until the late nineteenth century, when internal weakness and foreign interference led to Japan's political control and annexation of Korea as part of the Empire of Japan, in 1910. Japan ruled Korea as a colony until Japan's defeat in World War II, in 1945, ushered in the modern period of two Korean governments on the peninsula.[1]

Who ruled Korea before the division of the Peninsula in 1945?

Prior to the division of the Korean Peninsula in 1945, the Empire of Japan ruled Korea. Japan formally annexed Korea in 1910 and ruled Korea as its colony until Japan's defeat in World War II in 1945.

Japan reacted differently than most Asian powers that encountered Western nations and imperialism in the mid-nineteenth century. Japan launched its Meiji restoration, which rapidly modernized the country and saw the adoption of many Western attributes, including the use of modern military equipment and practices. Japan rose to become a regional power unparalleled by its Asian neighbors and pursued its imperial ambitions using the model of the Western imperial powers in Korea in the late nineteenth century. Japan defeated the Chinese in 1894–1895, in a war primarily fought over which great power would have influence over Korea. A decade later, Japan's defeat of Russia in a war in 1904–1905 solidified Japanese imperial ambitions with respect to Korea. In 1910, Japan eliminated Korea as an independent political entity by forcibly incorporating it into the Japanese empire.

A Korean proverb calls Korea a "shrimp among whales." It is a small country surrounded by larger ones. The late nineteenth and early twentieth centuries epitomize how the great powers fought over Korea as an object or prize, without reference to the will of the Korean people. The Joseon dynasty's political weakness contributed to the great powers' ability to disregard Korean leaders and the popular will, but the point that the larger powers did not defend Korean interests is a lasting memory that continues to animate Korean national consciousness and foreign and defense policies on both halves of the peninsula today. Japan's industrial investments in Korea, especially in the more mountainous northern half of the peninsula, and its business model created lasting economic legacies for Korea, but colonialism also tremendously distorted Korea's economy to benefit Japan.

Koreans widely resent Japan's colonization, which changed in its level of brutality after a failed Korean independence movement in 1919 and Japan's march to war in the 1930s. On January 8, 1918, US President Woodrow Wilson gave his "fourteen points" speech, which included a broad-minded call for self-determination. Individual nations should be able to determine their own political futures, and not be subject to the whims of empires, he proclaimed. In the following year, 1919, local Korean resistance to colonialism in line with Wilson's ideal culminated in the March 1 Movement demanding independence that swelled into mass protests. Japanese colonial administrators violently suppressed the movement.

In the 1920s, Japanese colonial administrators attempted to loosen their repression in some ways to avoid further rebellion and at the same time expanded its police and intelligence presence to root out Korean political activists before they could repeat something like the March 1 Movement. However, in the 1930s, Japanese colonialism grew substantially more brutal as Japan marched toward war and exploited its Korean colony in support of its militaristic goals. Japan's active attempts to repress Korean nationalism, language, and culture rose to new heights in the 1930s.

Japan expanded its war with China and a variety of Southeast Asian nations by attacking the United States at the Pearl Harbor military base in December 1941. The ill-fated move reversed Japan's war fortunes within months, which only increased its exploitation of Korean labor, economic outputs, and women. By 1944, Japan had mobilized almost four million Koreans to work outside their borders, including in Japan and Manchuria, to populate Japanese factories and mines. As Tokyo conscripted more Japanese men into its military, it used forced foreign labor to fill in the workforce. Imperial Japan also forced foreign women, mainly Koreans and Chinese, to service Japanese soldiers in brothels. Japan's recompense for this human rights violation during the war remains one of the sorest areas of Korea–Japan bilateral relations to this day. Significantly, the allied forces, particularly the United States and the Soviet Union, liberated Korea after Japan's defeat in World War II in August 1945, leading the great powers again to tremendously influence the division of the Korean Peninsula along a Cold War logic. Just as at the end of the Joseon dynasty and transition to Japanese colonialism, Koreans again would have a relatively minor voice in determining the political future of their country in 1945.

How did the Soviet Union influence the origins of North Korea?

The Soviet Union and the United States were uneasy allies at the end of World War II, brought together by common enemies. After Japan's surrender, the two emerging superpowers split Japan's Korean colony into two spheres of influence, the Soviets exerting influence in the north, and the Americans in the south. Moscow and Washington both looked for Koreans who could rule the country and remain loyal to them. In North Korea, a marginal guerilla leader, Kim Il Sung, traveled to Pyongyang, gained the backing of other Korean leaders in the northern half of the country, and won Moscow's support.

Moscow did not hand-pick Kim Il Sung to lead North Korea without reference to local political calculations, yet the Korean leader would show himself in the coming decades as one difficult to control. In other words, Kim Il Sung was more than simply Moscow's man in Pyongyang. However, the charismatic military and political leader assuaged the Soviets enough that they supported his rise to power in the 1940s. As the Cold War quickly deepened, the divided Korean Peninsula started to look more permanent even as the Pyongyang-based Korean government and the Seoul-based Korean government each claimed legitimacy over the entire peninsula. The two sides clashed in skirmishes in the late 1940s, and the two regimes formally claimed the establishment of their respective statehoods in virtually simultaneous and competing declarations in 1948. The Republic of Korea (ROK) in Seoul and Democratic People's Republic of Korea (DPRK) in Pyongyang were born.

An intense Korean nationalist, Kim Il Sung lobbied Soviet leader Joseph Stalin for military support and then permission to invade South Korea. Kim wanted to unify the Korean nation under his leadership and had the superior military forces to attempt it. Stalin finally relented and gave Kim his blessing but also urged Kim to coordinate with the Chinese leader Mao Zedong. Kim Il Sung launched the Korean War on June 25, 1950. It was completely his own initiative; however, great-power support had helped to create the conditions for his decision. In subsequent decades, Moscow would contribute to North Korea's economic and political development as a socialist ally. Kim was careful to safeguard his independence from his great-power benefactors while also seeking and receiving their material and political support throughout the Cold War and beyond.

How did the United States influence the origins of South Korea?

As the Soviets had done in the north, the United States played an instrumental role in the foundation of the ROK. South Korea's first president, Syngman Rhee, had lived most of his life before 1945 in the United States, and he arrived back in Korea after the Japanese surrender on an American military plane. While Rhee would soon come to show his deep differences with the United States in a variety of fields, he initially gained power and consolidated it around him based on his position as the leader backed by the American authorities.

Rhee was a fervent anticommunist, which was certainly a welcome attribute among the Americans at the time. He built a South Korean government focused on opposing the North Korean government and unifying the Korean nation under his leadership. Critically, the American leadership and Rhee helped craft the political institutions of the South Korean government, and Rhee was elected the republic's first president in 1948. When North Korea invaded in 1950, South Korea was ill prepared. Despite heroic and usually lethal efforts by South Korean forces to resist the much better equipped North Korean army, Pyongyang quickly captured Seoul and nearly pushed the South Korean army and small American military presence off the peninsula. American reinforcements stationed in Japan then intervened and changed the course of the war, saving the ROK from becoming a brief footnote in history. Fighting continued until an armistice was signed three years later.

After the armistice ended the main fighting in the Korean War, in 1953, the United States and the ROK signed a mutual defense treaty. The treaty allowed the United States to maintain a permanent military presence in South Korea, which continues to today. The expressed purpose of United States Forces Korea remains to deter and defend against North Korean aggression and uphold the United States' treaty commitments to the ROK. The United States also became central to South Korea's early economic development through trade and aid.

Who was North Korean leader Kim Il Sung?

Kim Il Sung was an uneducated guerilla fighter who opposed Japanese colonialism and rose to become the founder of North Korea. In the 1930s and 1940s, Kim Il Sung operated out of Manchuria, just north of the Korean Peninsula. He fought the Japanese colonialists on the margins of their power, which may help explain why he evaded capture, but he was significant enough as a frustrating element that the Japanese put a price on his head. He commanded up to three hundred fighters, but his regime would later exaggerate his importance in defeating Japanese colonialism.

After Japan's surrender in World War II and withdrawal from Korea, Kim Il Sung came to Pyongyang. A charismatic figure, he convinced enough of the disparate group of Koreans on the northern half of the peninsula to support him as one of North Korea's most important early leaders. For the next dozen years, throughout the Korean War and into the 1950s, Kim purged rivals and consolidated power. Other North Korean leaders, including leaders of the pro-Soviet and pro-Chinese factions, worried about the rising cult of personality that centered all political authority in Kim. They criticized Kim's launching of and conduct during the devastating Korean

War as well as his postwar economic policies. They attempted to oppose him in 1956 and failed. Kim carried out a massive purge, to Soviet and Chinese chagrin.

Purges would become a regular feature of Kim Il Sung's rule, as he rewarded loyalists, punished perceived and actual opponents, and set up a system of co-optation and repression characterized by inequality and human rights abuses. In a little over a decade, Kim Il Sung transformed North Korea from a dictatorship in which he was a top official among several important figures to a personalist regime in which he was equated with the regime.

Kim Il Sung began to transfer power to his eldest son, Kim Jong Il, in an extraconstitutional move in 1980. He started to withdraw from day-to-day governance duties, but when he died in 1994, he still formally held the top positions in all government, party, and military institutions. Kim Jong Il declared his father the "eternal president" after Kim Il Sung's death. Kim Il Sung created the Kim regime that is now in its third generation with his grandson, Kim Jong Un, running the country. Kim Il Sung is the most important person in the political history of the DPRK.

Who was South Korean President Syngman Rhee?

Syngman Rhee was a Korean nationalist, anticolonialist and anticommunist, and the first president of the ROK. Rhee was born in 1875. The Joseon dynasty was crumbling and foreign powers jockeying for influence over Korea in Rhee's formative years. He developed a strong sense of Korean nationalism and advocated for Korean independence, which in his youth landed him in a Japanese colonial jail for six years. Upon his release in 1904, he traveled to the United States and earned a bachelor's degree at George Washington University, a master's degree at Harvard, and a doctorate at Princeton. His dissertation, "Neutrality as Influenced by the United States," explored the basic philosophy that had undergirded American foreign policy from its founding in 1776 to 1872. He traveled briefly back to Korea in 1910, but then returned to the United States, where he remained for most of his life until 1945. Rhee had a deeper knowledge of both American culture and the US foreign policy orientation than any of his Korean contemporaries.

Rhee advocated Korean independence from Japan from his perch in the United States, while Kim Il Sung fought the Japanese colonialists more directly. The North Koreans would not lose the opportunity to highlight the contrast, calling Rhee and his government a lackey of the Americans. Starting in 1919, Rhee led the Korean Provisional Government in exile, and an American military plane returned him to Korea in 1945 after Japan's defeat. He quickly consolidated power by marginalizing other potential leaders in the southern half of the peninsula and, when the state was established in 1948, he was elected South Korea's first president.

Although initially elected to his post, Rhee took on increasing authoritarian traits. He ordered the extrajudicial imprisonment and execution of suspected communists during and after the Korean War. He opposed a 1953 ceasefire with North Korea, preferring to press onward to unify the Korean Peninsula under his leadership. He intimidated and undermined his political opponents to such an extent that it became difficult to continue to call the early ROK a democracy. Rhee resigned the presidency in 1960 under pressure and returned to Hawaii, where he died five years later.

How do the two Koreas view each other?

Although the inter-Korean relationship has become more dynamic since the 1990s, the broad history of the North Korea–South Korea interaction has been characterized as adversarial. Both Koreas claim in their constitutions to be the rightful government to rule over the entire Korean Peninsula.

Since their founding in 1948, the ROK and DPRK engaged in a violent and pervasive competition for legitimacy. The two Koreas fought a bloody three-year war from 1950 to 1953, backed by great-power supporters on both sides, but Koreans suffered the vast majority of the casualties and destruction. In the decades after the war, the two sides engaged in military clashes on land and sea, and North Korea made multiple assassination attempts on South Korean leaders and carried out terrorist attacks to discredit the ROK. The North Koreans claim the South Korean government is the "puppet" of the United States and not a true Korean government. The South Korean government portrays the North as a human-rights-abusing authoritarian regime that prioritizes expensive weapons systems over feeding its people. At least through the end of the Cold War, the two Korean governments overwhelmingly presented each other as enemies.

The inter-Korean relationship temporarily thawed at certain times during the Cold War and became more complex after the fall of the Soviet Union. For example, in 1972, representatives of the two Korean governments met and signed a joint communique in which they pledged to seek a "peaceful unification" that did not depend on foreign powers and agreed to undertake certain cultural exchanges and confidence-building measures. Spooked by the US–China diplomatic opening and, to a lesser extent, the US–Soviet détente that had relaxed the superpower tensions, Seoul and Pyongyang worried that their great-power benefactors might abandon them, and took actions into their own hands. In the 1980s, the two Koreas would again attempt a diplomatic rapprochement. However, these processes would peter out as the two authoritarian governments returned to confrontation.

In 1991, the ROK and the DPRK agreed in quick succession to join the United Nations. Previously, they had refused to join because both sought to represent Korea exclusively, and neither wanted to recognize the other as a legitimate state within the world body. In the 1980s, North Korean leader Kim Il Sung led the charge against mutual entry into the UN, noting that it would be a barrier to his ultimate goal of unifying Korea as a single state. But as the communist bloc collapsed, South Korea outpaced North Korea in terms of economic growth, political freedom, and possibly even conventional military prowess, Kim relented. Entry into the UN did not stop the two Koreas from criticizing the legitimacy of the other or alter either state's constitutional pursuit of unification, but it was an important step in recognizing the present reality of two Korean states.

In 1998, South Korea elected its first progressive president, who sought to revolutionize the inter-Korean relationship. Seeking to build habits of cooperation that he hoped would lead to a more permanent peace, South Korean President Kim Dae-jung accelerated political, cultural, humanitarian, and economic cooperation with North Korea. In 2000, he met with North Korean leader Kim Jong Il in the first inter-Korean summit. Building on a sense of Korean nationalism that transgressed borders, some South Korean progressives noted that the North Koreans should be understood as their "brothers" instead of their "enemies." South Korean conservatives labeled the effort naïve because North Korea continued to develop nuclear weapons and to maintain its military standoff against the South.

South Koreans may have had varied views of North Koreans during South Korea's military governments, but democratization in the late 1980s allowed that diversity of opinion to take more substantial political expression. In the democratic era, South Korean progressives in the presidential office could turn the divergent views of the North Koreans into national policy, whereas during the authoritarian era South Korean progressives were dissidents, who had relatively little ability to do so. In other words, South Korea's authoritarianism ensured stability in Seoul's North Korea policy. Democratization meant that South Korea's approach to its northern neighbor would oscillate given different preferred approaches among the South Korean electorate.

North Korea has not undergone democratization, and the same family has ruled the country since its founding with roughly similar tactics and strategic outlooks. Pyongyang oscillates in the level of vitriol articulated at the South Korean government. It generally preserves its tougher criticisms for South Korean conservatives, but it continues to attack the general legitimacy of the ROK to rule the South Korean people. North Korea highlights the continued US military presence in South Korea as evidence that the ROK is merely the puppet of the Americans, who wield the real political power in the country.

What does everyone need to know about the Korean War?

North Korea invaded South Korea on June 25, 1950. The fighting lasted three years until an armistice, or ceasefire, was signed on July 27, 1953. Casualties figures vary widely but it is estimated that at least three million civilians and soldiers died, including millions of Koreans, hundreds of thousands of Chinese, and tens of thousands of Americans. The Korean Peninsula is geographically about as long as the distance between Atlanta and Miami, and is about twice as wide as the Florida peninsula. As such, the intense fighting was concentrated in a small space.

North Korea had lobbied the Soviets extensively for military aid and political support ahead of Kim Il Sung's decision to invade South Korea. Although American officials at the time widely suspected that the Kremlin was behind the North Korean invasion, archival evidence shows definitively that Kim Il Sung had pushed the invasion idea with Stalin, who finally relented.

North Korea enjoyed early military success after the invasion. Its military forces were far superior to those of South Korea. South Korean soldiers were so desperate that they resorted to extremely risky tactics, such as running up to a tank to drop a grenade inside, to try to slow the North Korean advance. They lacked their own tanks to match the North Korean tanks on the battlefield. Within three days, North Korea had captured the South's capital, Seoul. By the end of the summer of 1950, the North Korean forces had driven across most of the peninsula. The American and South Korean forces defended the southeast corner of the peninsula around the Korean port city of Pusan, in what became called "the Pusan perimeter."

In September 1950, American General Douglas MacArthur, stationed in Tokyo, orchestrated a massive amphibious landing behind North Korean enemy lines. The Incheon landing on Korea's west coast, near Seoul, was the first turning point in the war. The US and ROK forces liberated Seoul and pushed north across the entirety of North Korean territory to the Korean border with China.

MacArthur had judged that China would not intervene in the war, but it did. Chinese intervention in October 1950 was the second turning point in the war, and it drove the US and ROK forces back down the peninsula. In 1951, the two sides reached a stalemate, but fighting would continue for another two years until they signed an armistice, separating the two Koreas at roughly the same point as when the war began.

The fighting in the Korean War ended with an American general and representatives of China and North Korea signing an armistice. South Korea refused to participate because the South Korean president wanted to continue the fight for unification and continued to advocate for this with the Americans throughout the 1950s. A ceasefire is a temporary instrument, but the Korean one evolved into a permanent arrangement; to this day the relevant parties have still failed to agree on a peace treaty to end the war formally.

What is the United Nations Command?

After North Korea invaded South Korea, the UN Security Council condemned the action and urged UN member states to help repel the aggression. A unified military command, which operated under the UN flag and was led by an American general, organized various countries' military contributions to repel North Korea's invasion. The United Nations Command remains in effect today.

North Korea invaded South Korea on June 25, 1950 and two days later, the UN Security Council issued UN Security Council Resolution 83 calling the North Korean action a breach of peace. The council recommended that member states provide South Korea with support to repel the attack. Two weeks later, on July 7, the UN Security Council issued Resolution 84. It urged the states sending forces to Korea to repel North Korea's invasion and "make such forces and other assistance available to a unified command under the United States of America." The resolution requested that the United States designate a military commander and authorized the use of the UN flag for the military operations.[2]

In 1950, the UN Security Council was still in its infancy. The Soviets had a veto-wielding permanent seat on the body, but China did not have one at the time. Protesting an unrelated matter, the Soviets boycotted UN Security Council votes, including those on the UN Security Council resolutions authorizing a UN call to arms to respond to North Korea's invasion, which enabled the passage of the UN resolutions. The top American general in South Korea today retains three titles: Commander of the United States Forces Korea, of the (US-ROK) Combined Forces Command, and of the United Nations Command. The UN flag flies every day in front of the commander's headquarters in the middle of Seoul.

Beyond the United States and South Korea, fifteen UN member states sent troops to Korea to fight the DPRK and communist expansion. The UN "sending states" retain a special role on the Korean Peninsula today, and several keep a very small token military presence in South Korea. At the peak, the fifteen states provided just over 4 percent of the entire UN Command's troops, which were dominated by ROK and US service personnel.[3] Nevertheless, the UN Command conferred an international legitimacy on the US-ROK effort that continues to irk the North Koreans today.

Why does the North Korean government hate the United States?

The North Korean government calls the United States an imperialist power, propping up the ROK and thwarting North Korea's effort to unify the Korean Peninsula. The North Koreans maintain that they would have unified Korea by force in 1950 if the United States had not intervened militarily to stop it, and they are probably right on this score. While North Korea laments the American intervention, South Korea heralds it. North Korea maintained superior military forces than the South Korean military for most of the Cold War, but Pyongyang could not defeat the US-ROK alliance. In the North Korean view, the United States not only frustrated its main goal of unifying the Korean nation in 1950 but also continually thwarted this effort for decades.

Pyongyang continues to blame Washington for a variety of its social and economic problems, pointing to US sanctions and military pressure as the root of North Korean economic problems and the reason for its highly militarized society. North Korean leader Kim Il Sung came to power fighting Japanese imperialism, and the United States replaced Japan as the main foreign enemy that helped provide the raison d'être for the DPRK. Anti-imperialism and unification are two central pillars that have motivated North Korea's intensely nationalistic ideology from its founding to today, and the United States' purported hostility toward North Korea is central to both narratives.

The North Korean government actively vilifies the United States and tries to create a society deeply hostile to the United States. Complaints about American imperialism are a daily occurrence in North Korean state media. They leverage everything from history to current events with facts real and imagined to bolster this anti-imperialist outlook. North Korea's state-run education system teaches hate. "Hate" is a strong word, but it is justified in this case. Pyongyang instills a deep anti-Americanism in its populace from cradle to grave.

On history, the North Koreans point to the immense destruction leveled at North Korea during the Korean War and to American human rights abuses in the conduct of the war, including air strikes that claimed military and civilian lives. The North Koreans buttress these claims by noting—falsely—that they did not initiate the war. North Korea seizes on news of crimes or tragic accidents by American service personnel stationed in South Korea as evidence of a South Korean government that is acting as a lackey of the Americans and failing to defend the dignity of the Korean people. The North Korean government also utilizes racist depictions of Americans to deepen the hatred toward them.[4]

Why did the Korean War never officially end?

After three years of fighting that claimed the lives of millions of Koreans, hundreds of thousands of Chinese, and tens of thousands of Americans, major hostilities on the Korean Peninsula came to an end. Neither side won a decisive military victory on the battlefield, but both sides tried to maximize their political outcomes at the negotiating table. Zero-sum trade-offs in each side's core demands, mixed with a dose of early Cold War ideological imperatives, almost foreordained failure for the peace talks.

Major movements in the Korean War took place in the first year of the conflict. North Korea nearly pushed the American and South Korean forces off the peninsula in the summer of 1950, and US and South Korean forces pushed the North Koreans all the way back to North Korea's northern border with China by year's end. China's intervention in the war on behalf of the North Koreans reversed the tide yet again as the two sides met in the middle of the peninsula, where the war initially started. The last two years of the war saw stalemate, and the two sides tried to negotiate a ceasefire on their own terms.

The Chinese and Soviets began discussing the possibility of an armistice with each other as early as December 1950, and North Korean leader Kim Il Sung had voiced his support for it to the Soviets and the Chinese by June 1951, declassified records show. The United States formally proposed an armistice on June 28, 1951. North Korea and its allies agreed in principle to the idea. However, Stalin continued to urge the continuation of the North Korean war effort despite the protracted stalemate until his death in March 1953. Following Stalin's death, the Soviets and North Koreans agreed to negotiate a conclusion of the fighting.[5] South Korean President Syngman Rhee was the last holdout and publicly rejected the armistice agreement shortly before its signature.[6] Nevertheless, two generals—one representing the United States Army and the UN Command—and another representing the (North) Korean People's Army and the Chinese People's Volunteers—signed a ceasefire on July 27, 1953. Except as a member of the UN Command, South Korea notably was not represented in the agreement.

The armistice was meant to be temporary until a formal peace treaty could be finalized. In 1954, the great powers met for the Geneva Conference to discuss a variety of international issues, including "the Korea question." The United States and China did not want South Korea and North Korea, respectively, to break ranks with their advocacy, but this was primarily a great-power negotiation over the future of the Korean Peninsula. The talks went nowhere. The positions were so far apart that the US negotiating team later recollected that its only goals were to determine the composition of who would attend the peace talks and to set up a time and place to negotiate the substantive issues. The two sides could not even do that. Cold War politics handicapped the Americans in talking with the Chinese, and the Chinese likewise suffered from ideological barriers, making progress even less likely. The Geneva Conference ended up focusing more on France's extraction from Vietnam, as there was no movement on Korea. In subsequent decades, the two sides would meet to discuss a peace treaty, but they never reached agreement and the temporary armistice has remained since 1953.

2

KOREA'S HOT WAR TURNS COLD

KOREA IN THE COLD WAR

What is the Juche *philosophy of self-reliance?*

In 1955, North Korean leader Kim Il Sung delivered a major speech that introduced the world to the *Juche* idea. Coming just seven years after the establishment of the DPRK, two years after the Korean War ceasefire, and amid continued efforts by Kim Il Sung to consolidate his power at home and establish his cult of personality, Kim defined an idea that would guide all political decisions in his regime.

At its core, *Juche* was about extreme Korean nationalism. *Juche*, or "self-reliance," hoped to preserve the leader's discretion in foreign affairs by making him subject to no one. The Chinese forces that had saved Kim Il Sung's North Korea from military defeat in the Korean War were still in North Korea. Kim Il Sung's nationalism and self-reliance philosophy would insist on their withdrawal. A malleable philosophy that shifted to fit the needs of the leader, *Juche* sought to guide governmental decisions and citizens' personal behavior as well. The all-encompassing idea hoped to motivate each North Korean's life to create a righteous and moral, self-reliant nation.

North Korea was an entity of Koreans for Koreans. It blamed the nation's woes on foreign imperialism. The great powers around the Korean Peninsula had trampled on the interests of the Korean people throughout their history, as seen most recently and vividly at the time with Japanese colonialism and the peninsula's post–World War II division. Only through a militarily and ideologically strong state could the DPRK achieve its grand purpose of protecting Korean sovereignty.

Juche conveniently juxtaposed the North Korean and South Korean systems to assert the moral superiority of the North Korean model of governance. Kim Il Sung noted that South Korea was reliant on the United States in a way that North Korea was not dependent on its own patrons. South Korea accepted the permanent stationing of US troops on its soil. That, combined with American economic aid, North Korea maintained, made foreign influence so strong in Seoul that the South Korean government was simply a puppet of the Americans, who were pulling all the strings. The United States was not seeking to protect the interests of the Korean people, and its involvement was just another example of a foreign imperialist exploiting Koreans for its own ends. Pyongyang would stand up to the United States and its puppet government in Seoul.

The *Juche* idea extended well beyond high politics and issues of national security. North Korea heralded "our style," or "Korean-style," socialism. The Kim regime, not Marx, Lenin, or contemporary leaders in Moscow or Beijing, would define the country's system. *Juche* agriculture meant that North Korea, a country with little arable land, would seek to grow most of its own food. North Korea did not want to rely on foreign powers for security or imports, including food imports. Sanctions would further reinforce the North Korean conviction that economic self-reliance insulated the country from undue foreign pressure. *Juche* art would help propagandize the country with politically correct movies, novels, and festivals to instill a deeper sense of the revolution in citizens' everyday lives.

The Korean Workers' Party was charged with guiding not only government policy but also the conduct of people's everyday lives. The all-encompassing *Juche* ideology provided both kinds of guidance. Pragmatic expertise was valued less than this moral guidance to construct a new kind of country and society. Kim led the Korean Workers' Party in the 1950s and later carved out a position for himself that put him above the party completely. From this perch, he was the ultimate arbiter of ideological correctness and set the standard for what was righteous, good, and best for the individual and the country. His supposedly sage and benevolent leadership and vague and flexible nationalism under the *Juche* banner meant that Kim could direct social, political, and economic life in North Korea as he saw fit and gain a degree of buy-in from his government and society through this ideology.

How did Kim Il Sung consolidate his power?

When Japanese colonialism in Korea abruptly ended in 1945 with Tokyo's defeat in World War II, Kim Il Sung was one of several aspiring Korean leaders who descended on Pyongyang to vie for power. In the Soviet-occupied northern half of the peninsula, a relationship with Moscow was necessary but insufficient to lead. A Korean leader in northern Korea required some domestic support too. Indeed, it is not uncommon in situations like these for great powers to seek to back a leader who is supportive of their interests but moderated by the need to be domestically viable as well. Kim had that combination of acceptability to Moscow and sufficient credibility among northern Koreans. With a dose of luck and political skill, Kim Il Sung's stature rose internally. With this combination of degrees of domestic and Soviet backing, he took the position of premier upon the founding of the state in 1948.

In the second half of the 1940s, Kim Il Sung was the most important political leader in North Korea. However, he did not control every significant political grouping of leaders or citizens. The new country was rife with factions. Kim Il Sung was loyal to his peculiar group of guerrilla fighters, who had operated against Japanese colonialism in the 1930s and early 1940s out of Manchuria, just north of the Korean Peninsula.

Communists from southern Korea who formed the South Korea Workers' Party also moved to Pyongyang. Koreans who lived and organized in China during the Japanese colonial period and headquartered in the Chinese city of Yanan made up another group. And those who had lived and trained in the Soviet Union were yet another faction. These groups numbered in the hundreds because most Koreans were not actively political in this way. Kim Il Sung did not win over the competing factions. Rather, he purged them in just over a decade.[1]

The Korean War provided an easy excuse to purge domestic opponents under the guise of punishing traitors. Communists who previously operated in southern Korea were prime targets because they could be associated—fairly or not—with the DPRK's rival government and contemporary enemy at war in Seoul. Kim Il Sung invented plausible excuses during the war to purge factionalists. After American General Douglas MacArthur landed at Incheon and pushed the North Korean forces back to the Chinese border before Beijing entered the war, the US–South Korean forces occupied northern Korea for a few months. In late 1950, Kim Il Sung accused factionalists of collaborating with the enemy during this time in order to purge these domestic opponents. At the conclusion of the fighting in 1953, Kim Il Sung again created a story about the South Korea Workers' Party in order to execute several of its top leaders.

During the 1950–1953 Korean War, Moscow and Beijing had more pull with Kim Il Sung than they would in subsequent years. Moscow provided much of the early military and economic aid along with political support for Kim Il Sung's war. Beijing's military intervention saved North Korea from extinction, and hundreds of thousands of Chinese soldiers paid the ultimate price. Kim Il Sung was in a poor position to try to purge the North Korean groups with the deepest links to the Soviet Union and China at this time.

Kim Il Sung was a bold risk-taker, and he decided after the end of fighting in 1953 to continue his campaign toward uncontested leadership in North Korea. He appeared to judge that the threat of alienating his foreign backers was less concerning than the benefit to him of eliminating domestic opponents. In large meetings of the Korean Workers' Party, in 1953 and 1956, North Korean factionalists tried to criticize Kim. This was the era of de-Stalinization in the communist world, and Moscow, at least, favored moving away from the overwhelming and oppressive rule of a strongman leader like the Soviet Union's Joseph Stalin toward a broader representation of North Korea's Communist Party. Kim Il Sung had no interest in the de-Stalinization message from Moscow and stage-managed a response to his critics. He expelled some officials from the party and exiled or executed others.

Moscow and Beijing were concerned. They sent a rare joint diplomatic delegation to Pyongyang to protest and to warn Kim to stop. The Korean Workers' Party officially claimed that it had reversed course, but Kim's purges continued until, by the end of the 1950s, he had destroyed the pro-China (Yanan) and pro-Soviet factions in North Korean politics. Kim Il Sung had already promulgated his *Juche* philosophy of nationalistic self-reliance, and he could cite the Korean factions with links to China and the Soviet Union as less purely advancing Korean national interest. Intense nationalism and ruthless power politics were central to Kim Il Sung's consolidation of power.

What was North Korea's early relationship with the Soviet Union?

The Soviet Union was the DPRK's political, economic, and military patron in the early Cold War, but there was no love lost between the two countries. The relationship would hold together because of the perceived geopolitical necessities stimulated by the Cold War, but Moscow–Pyongyang relations had soured significantly by the mid-1950s. Pyongyang relied on Moscow for political and material support, but Moscow also depended on Pyongyang as a bulwark against Korean unification in the American orbit.

As World War II allies against Imperial Japan in the Pacific Theater (as well as Nazi Germany and fascist Italy in Europe), the United States and the Soviet Union occupied Korea after Japan's defeat. The makeshift allies quickly turned into Cold War adversaries, and the two superpowers looked for controllable and locally sustainable Korean leaders. Neither superpower was wholly successful. If the Soviets could have foreseen Kim Il Sung's future efforts to curtail their influence and buck their demands, Moscow may have intervened differently in the 1940s. Nevertheless, they ended up with a leader who would erode Soviet influence but maintain a mantle of communism and genuine anti-Americanism in North Korea.

Moscow initially tried to influence Pyongyang as it did its Eastern European satellite states. In the 1940s and early 1950s, a Soviet senior adviser resided in every North Korean ministry. Moscow called these men the Soviet "ministers," meaning they were basically expected to direct each North Korean government organ. Soviet officials were also implanted in every North Korean state-run business and military unit. Kim Il Sung would do away with these positions, expel most foreigners, and limit contact between North Koreans and Russians.

Kim Il Sung's purge of factionalists, meaning those North Korean political leaders without unquestioned loyalty to Kim, accelerated in 1956. When factionalists attempted to speak out against Kim Il Sung's cult of personality, including Kim's personal domination of North Korean politics, Kim responded by pushing them out of positions of power, expelling them from the country, or executing them. Critically, this included officials with ties to Moscow. Kim largely completed this purge of North Korean factional political leaders by the end of the 1950s.

In the 1960s, Kim moved to more thoroughly isolate any remaining pro-Soviet group members in North Korean society. Soviet women who had married North Korean men were not allowed to return to North Korea after visits to the Soviet Union, or the regime transferred the Korean husbands to remote parts of North Korea that lacked adequate facilities for families. When this marital harassment was insufficient, the regime forced couples to divorce and eliminated mail service to keep them from contacting each other later.[2] Kim Il Sung expunged pro-Soviet groups in both North Korean politics and society.

Nevertheless, geopolitics held the two countries together. Moscow voiced its displeasure about Pyongyang's policies and even limited aid, but the Soviets never cut off the North Koreans until the end of the Cold War. Soviet economic aid had helped fuel North Korea's economic revitalization and industrialization after the Korean War. Soviet military aid and even reluctant civilian nuclear assistance helped the country to build and maintain a formidable fighting force and later construct nuclear weapons. Pyongyang was not reliably pro-Soviet, but it was reliably anti-American. For Moscow during the Cold War, that would have to suffice.

What was North Korea's early relationship with China?

The China–North Korea relationship was supposed to be as close as "lips and teeth," especially during the early Cold War period. In reality, it never was. The two East Asian communist countries had a powerful claim to fraternal solidarity, including the provision of troops to aid each other's war efforts in the late 1930s to early 1950s, but the suspicion of Kim Il Sung's government of the pro-China (Yanan) faction in North Korean politics and its nationalistic emphasis on self-reliance created a more transactional relationship that ebbed and flowed as it served the two regimes' interests.

In the late 1930s and early 1940s, Mao Zedong led an army of Chinese communists in fighting a civil war against the Chinese nationalists. Both Chinese forces militarily opposed Imperial Japan's intervention in China to varying degrees. At this time, a group of Korean communists traveled to the Chinese Communist Party's then capital of Yanan to join in the fight. In the late 1940s, communist North Korea also gave rear area refuge to the Chinese communist forces later in Mao's war effort. If the Yanan faction of pro-China Korean communists who fought with Mao in the Chinese Civil War had ruled North Korea, the China–North Korea relationship may have developed differently. But this faction was just one of several in the early years of the DPRK, and Kim Il Sung was not a member of it.

When Kim Il Sung was planning to reunify the Korean Peninsula under his leadership and build up the necessary military strength to conquer the South, he intensely engaged the Soviets. Only at Soviet leader Joseph Stalin's prodding did Kim Il Sung finally discuss the matter with Chinese leader Mao Zedong, a few weeks before Kim's invasion in June 1950. The summer military campaign went well for Kim, but American reinforcements pushed North Korean forces back to the Chinese border. Mao's decision in October 1950 to send Chinese People's Volunteers, who were Chinese soldiers by a different name, saved Kim Il Sung. It did not engender lasting North Korean gratitude.

During the Korean War, North Korea and China disagreed on a variety of issues ranging from military tactics to command relationships. After the war, Kim demanded the withdrawal of all foreign forces from Korean soil, meaning that he told the Chinese troops that they were no longer welcome and needed to go home. In 1956, Kim launched a major purge of pro-China and pro-Soviet factionalists, to Beijing's and Moscow's dismay. Kim purged the pro-China Yanan faction, the very group of Korean communists who had fought alongside Mao through the Chinese Civil War. The more general claim of a fraternal relationship between the North Koreans and Chinese did not fully apply to the group of North Koreans running the government under Kim.

China–North Korea relations soured, but Soviet–North Korea relations nosedived. Kim sought to increase his personal hold over North Korean politics precisely as the Soviet leadership moved in the opposite direction. After Soviet leader Joseph Stalin's death in 1953, his successor, Nikita Khrushchev, wanted to limit the power of a single communist leader in the Soviet Union and the accompanying severe repression. He expected Soviet satellites to follow suit. Kim had no intention of complying.

As China's relationship with the Soviet Union grew increasingly tense in what is called the Sino-Soviet split, North Korea played the two communist giants off against each other. North Korea grew closer to China in the early 1960s, because the relationship with the Soviet Union had fallen further. This would only reverse itself midway through the decade as China embarked on the radical and disastrous social experiment called the Cultural Revolution. A byproduct of the Chinese Cultural Revolution's ideological push included criticism of Kim's model of governance, which encouraged Kim to move away from China and back toward the Soviets.[3] The early China–North Korea relationship was transactional, lacked the foundation based on values or ideology the two sides occasionally claimed, and oscillated as a result.

Why did the United States and South Korea sign a mutual defense treaty?

The United States and South Korea signed a mutual defense treaty on October 1, 1953, just a few months after American, North Korean, and Chinese representatives had signed an armistice ending the fighting in the Korean War. The mutual defense treaty explicitly noted the two allies' intent to deter invasions by other external aggressors. In practice, it was a message to North Korea and its superpower partners that another invasion of South Korea would be met by another US defensive response. The South Korean government granted the United States military the right to base troops in South Korea. And the United States Senate, giving its advice and consent, ratified the treaty in 1954 on the inscribed condition that the

United States would only come to South Korea's aid if North Korea started the fight.[4]

The treaty established the US–South Korea military alliance that remains today. The United States promised to come to South Korea's defense in the event of another North Korean invasion of South Korea. South Korea likewise promised in this mutual defense treaty to come to America's aid if it was attacked, but the weak and vulnerable South Korean state in 1953 had little wherewithal to do so. The treaty served US security by limiting the perceived threat of the expansion of global communism from this particular part of the globe. But though South Korea gained an American defense commitment, its political leadership sought more.

South Korean President Syngman Rhee was a committed anticommunist, wanted to reunify the Korean nation under his leadership just as Kim Il Sung did, and hoped to get American troops to help in this cause. No South Korean representative signed the 1953 armistice because Rhee wanted to continue the fight. The American president at the time, Dwight Eisenhower, by contrast, had campaigned on a platform that included ending the war. Rhee dissented publicly with Eisenhower ahead of the armistice and tried to undermine the negotiations. Rhee quelled his opposition to the armistice in exchange for the defense-treaty negotiations that Rhee hoped would bind Washington to his unification enterprise. In ratifying the agreement, the US Senate put in writing that "neither party is obligated, under article III of the above Treaty, to come to the aid of the other except in the case of an external armed attack against such party."[5] In other words, the United States had no desire to get pulled into another Korean War that its South Korean ally had started. The treaty note was only a part of the United States effort to restrain Rhee from trying to move north.[6]

The treaty also established the legal grounds to base American troops in South Korea. Article IV says in its entirety, "The Republic of Korea grants, and the United States of America accepts, the right to dispose United States land, air and sea forces in and about the territory of the Republic of Korea as determined by mutual agreement."[7] American troops reside in South Korea, not as occupying force, but at the invitation of the South Korean government. Seoul can terminate this basing right at any time, and the United States can also decide to withdraw its forces. There is nothing in the treaty that precludes such a change, and it would not affect the legal commitment to guarantee the other country's defense. This provision would become more relevant in later decades as the South Korean military forces grew more sophisticated, and American leaders at times urged a reduction or even an elimination of the permanent stationing of US troops in South Korea. Article IV does not indicate that the American troops in South Korea can only be used to repel North Korean aggression, raising controversy in South Korea in more recent years on whether South Korea should allow the American troops on its soil to be part of a broader regional defense against a rising China too.

Who was South Korean President Park Chung-hee?

Park Chung-hee was a South Korean general, president, and dictator. He grew increasingly repressive over the course of his eighteen-year tenure leading South Korea, but he remains popular in South Korea today for developing South Korea's economy. Although South Korean politics shifted from moderately repressive under Syngman Rhee to highly repressive under Park, he also catapulted South Korea from an impoverished country reliant on agriculture to an advanced industrial economy.

Born in 1917 during Japanese colonial rule of Korea, Park attended a Japanese military academy and served in the Japanese army during World War II. His domestic opponents noted this with disdain, but the North Koreans focused on it. North Korean leader Kim Il Sung made a name for himself as an anti-Japan guerilla fighter trying to reclaim Korean independence at precisely the time when Park was fighting for the Japanese. Koreans in the north and the south revile the Japanese colonialism, so North Korean arguments that Park had been a Japanese "collaborator" in the past and was a "puppet" of the American imperialists at the time of his rule had some bite.

After South Korea's first president, Syngman Rhee, resigned under pressure and left the country in 1960, Yun Po Son was elected president. He stayed in office for less than a year before General Park Chung-hee led a successful coup, deposing Yun in 1961. General Park was elected president two years later. He won subsequent elections after harassing opponents and the media and expanding his personal control over key South Korean institutions, including business and the intelligence apparatus. In 1972, Park declared martial law and promulgated a new South Korean constitution called the "Yushin constitution," which was best known for its increased political repression.

Park was a conservative anticommunist who retained the support of his American ally despite particularly intense difficulties in the US–South Korea alliance near the end of his rule. In 1965, he established diplomatic relations with Japan. The United States welcomed this improved relationship between its two northeast Asian allies, but the move was controversial for Park at home. Beyond the general unpopularity of Japan in Korea, Park's history of serving in the Japanese military during the colonial era made this decision even more difficult for him from a domestic political perspective. However, establishing diplomatic relations with Japan also meant that Tokyo would provide Seoul with hundreds of millions of dollars of grants and loans. This was a substantial sum at the time for a developing country, and it helped fuel the economic development and industrialization plan that has been Park's most lasting positive legacy. South Korea's tremendous economic development stemmed from a variety of factors, including the government's economic policy, hard work and sacrifice from Korean workers, and American aid—but also Japan's grants and loans after the two countries established diplomatic relations.

Under Park, South Korea's per capita gross domestic product (GDP) rose from $93 in the first year of his rule to $1,773 in the last year of his rule.[8] National wealth was far from evenly distributed, and South Korea was not yet wealthy. However, Park transformed South Korea forever and provided a particularly compelling contrast between the North and South Korean forms of governance in providing for the material needs of its people.

Notwithstanding his anticommunism, Park showed a willingness to negotiate with the North Koreans when necessary. His government negotiated with North Korea the first inter-Korean joint communique in 1972. The two Koreas were worried about their great-power backers abandoning them, especially after President Richard Nixon went to China, and Washington and Beijing established diplomatic relations. The Koreas worried that their patrons would pursue their own interests whether it was good for their Korean allies or not. After the American withdrawal from Vietnam and the collapse of the South Vietnamese government, Seoul further worried that it could be next if Washington withdrew from Korea too.

North–South relations did not advance much because inter-Korean negotiations quickly broke down. In 1974, a pro–North Korea man who lived in Japan traveled to South Korea to assassinate Park. Park was delivering a speech; the assailant fired widely, missing his target but hitting Park's wife, South Korea's first lady. After the gunshot had critically injured his wife, who would soon die from her wound, the stoic Park returned to the podium and completed his speech. Park Chung-hee's daughter, Park Geun-hye, would take on many of the former ceremonial responsibilities of her late mother. The South Korean electorate decades later elected the younger Park president.

Worried about defending his country against a militarily superior North Korea if the United States withdrew from South Korea as it did from South Vietnam, Park initiated South Korea's own secret nuclear weapons program in the 1970s. He tried to keep it hidden from the United States, but American intelligence learned about the nuclear effort. The two sides deeply disagreed about the wisdom of South Korea's pursuing nuclear weapons, which soured US–South Korean ties.

The United States also criticized Park's increasingly repressive government, especially after his declaration of martial law and imposition of the Yushin constitution in 1972. In the 1976 American presidential election, candidate Jimmy Carter called for the withdrawal of US forces in South Korea, in part based on Park's human rights abuses. President Gerald Ford assured Park that he would not withdraw American troops, but Carter defeated Ford in the election. On Carter's inauguration in 1977, he moved to end the US military presence in South Korea. Carter never completed the effort, but it remained a major sticking point in US–South Korean relations until Park's death in 1979.

In 1979, Park's long-time aide and spy chief assassinated him. Another South Korean general, Chun Doo-hwan, took control of the government after a brief interregnum, terminated Park's nuclear weapons program, and advanced a US–South Korean conventional military build-up with President Ronald Reagan. By the end of the 1980s, Park's authoritarian politics had given way to democratization, but his legacy was secured for stimulating South Korea's tremendous economic rise that continued in the years after his death.

What was the South Korean economic "Miracle on the Han"?

After the Korean War, South Korea sought to industrialize and develop its economy. Its impressive success in bringing about rapid economic growth was dubbed the "Miracle on the Han" for the Han River that runs through Seoul.

During the Japanese colonial era (1910–1945), the Japanese built industrial facilities in the northern, more mountainous part of Korea and relied on agriculture in the southern part of Korea, where more land was suitable for farming. This gave North Korea an initial industrial advantage over South Korea when the peninsula was first divided after World War II. However, South Korean leaders after the Korean War decided to invest in specific industrial sectors for export. They would rely on the money they earned from trade to supply their other needs in what became a textbook example of export-led industrialization.

The South Korean people worked hard and sacrificed to enjoy the fruits of their investments, but their authoritarian political leaders had given them no choice. Some have argued South Korea's success shows the wisdom of benign authoritarian leaders' promoting economic development that may not be popular or deemed politically possible in a democracy. After a country develops economically under authoritarianism, it can democratize later. Evidence from other countries and a changed global economy would moderate the enthusiasm for this argument, but South Korea's economic development revolutionized the country before democracy took root. South Korea also received significant development aid from both the United States and, later, Japan, which helped fuel its "miracle."

South Korea's economic-development model favored big business, which remains a feature of its economy today. Some of the country's largest firms are the most well known internationally, including Samsung, Hyundai, and LG. Others, such as the energy and telecommunications conglomerate SK, construction and hospitality conglomerate Lotte, and the steel giant POSCO, are perhaps less well known outside Korea or apart from industry specialists but remain important economically. South Korea's mega-conglomerates got their start or grew significantly during the economic miracle with close South Korean government support.

South Korea's economy saw advances in the 1950s as the country recovered from the depths of the Korean War, but the economic growth really started in the 1960s and continued until the mid-1990s. The growth of South Korea's large conglomerates in tandem with government support gave way to the increasing forces of globalization in the mid- and late 1990s. Calls for economic reforms to adjust South Korea's big business–government relationship heightened as South Korea saw a sudden economic downturn.[9] South Korea recovered economically and showed that its place among the world's advanced industrial economies was secure.

How and when did South Korea overtake North Korea economically?

South Korea overtook North Korea economically in the 1970s. Some economic historians argue that Seoul may have started outpacing Pyongyang as early as the 1960s, but the leaders of the two Koreas became aware of South Korea's economic superiority in the late 1970s and dated the switchover to earlier in that decade. In terms of the inter-Korean political competition, Seoul could start to feel more confident about the relative merits of its economic model to the North Korean one in the 1970s.

It is often surprising to non-Korea specialists that North Korea ever could have faster economic growth than South Korea. South Korea today is known for its modern economy, its Samsung smartphones and LG TVs being regular favorites among Western consumers, while the news about North Korea centers on its inability to feed its own people and features pictures of ox-drawn farming equipment. But North Korea had several economic advantages over South Korea after the Korean War. The Japanese colonial government focused on industrial investments in the mountainous northern part of the peninsula and on agriculture in the flatter southern part. Industry allowed for faster economic growth, and North Korea needed to rebuild existing industrial infrastructure after the Korean War rather than start anew as South Korea did. Hydroelectric plants built during the Japanese era continue to provide electricity in North Korea today and are one example of the inherited legacy of Japan's economic investments.

Communism also had some initial economic benefits that would later turn into liabilities. Land reform and mobilizing North Korean workers in a forced and organized way allowed North Korea to rebuild quickly. The Soviets also provided North Korea significant development aid that shaped its economy in a way that remains relevant today. In the early decades, the North Koreans presented their economic model as the one that provided for the Korean people better than did that of the South Korean economy.

The returns on these North Korean investments stagnated as South Korea's model saw greater benefits. It became more obvious to leaders in Seoul, Pyongyang, and beyond by the late 1970s that South Korea's economic model was winning out. The gap would grow so immense during the 1980s that by the end of the decade, North Korea could not credibly hope to catch up. Today, South Korea's economy is twenty-two times larger than North Korea's economy on a per capita basis.[10]

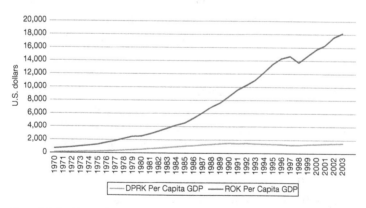

Figure 2.1 North Korea–South Korea Real GDP Per Capita, 1970–2003.

Source: Maddison Historical Statistics, University of Groningen, January 11, 2018, https://www. rug.nl/ggdc/historicaldevelopment/maddison/.

How did the two Koreas participate in the Vietnam War?

South Korea and North Korea contributed to opposite sides of the Vietnam War. South Korea sent ground troops to support the US-backed South Vietnam, while North Korea provided fighter jet pilots to support the communist government in North Vietnam. North Vietnamese regular forces were supported by pro–North Vietnam guerilla groups, and South Korea suspected that North Korea would seek to employ pro–North Korean guerilla groups in case of another Korean war.

Despite real differences between Vietnam and Korea, the similarities were sufficient to encourage the two Koreas to draw parallels to their own situation. Neither Korea wanted to see the other side's Vietnamese government win the war, but they also did not want to divert too many of their own military resources in fighting a bloody war in a far-off place that did not directly affect their own security.

The Korean contributions to the Vietnam War were born in part out of a recognized parallel to their own situation, but more so out of requests from their patrons. Washington encouraged Seoul to send troops to support South Vietnam's effort, and Moscow and Beijing encouraged Pyongyang to provide support to North Vietnam. Both sides were eager to withdraw their military contributions once the great powers signaled their own waning support for the long conflict.

As American popular support for the Vietnam War eroded and American leaders sought the withdrawal of US forces from the fight, Seoul became increasingly worried that Washington might do something similar in Korea. Seoul worried the United States might give up on South Korea, as it perceived the United States had given up on South Vietnam, if American expenses or casualties in protecting South Korea became too onerous.

Specifically, President Richard Nixon gave an impromptu press conference in Guam in 1969 that rattled South Korea. He called on Asian states to do more to provide for their own security. The United States would continue to honor its alliance commitments against Soviet meddling and to offer the American nuclear umbrella, but Asian states would have to bear more of the burden of their own defense. His comments were focused on South Vietnam, but he also mentioned South Korea. The press conference gave birth to what became known as the Nixon Doctrine.

The American military withdrawal from South Vietnam precipitated North Vietnamese leader Ho Chi Minh's unification of Vietnam by force. The North Vietnamese tortured and executed former South Vietnamese leaders as South Vietnamese refugees fled the country en masse. South Korea did not want to see the same happen to it, and President Carter's advocacy of a complete US military withdrawal from South Korea just one year after the fall of South Vietnam further worried Seoul. The events in Vietnam encouraged North Korea in the 1970s and worried South Korea. In the context of insecurity in the 1970s, the South Korean government resorted to extreme actions, including trying to bribe members of Congress to support keeping US troops in South Korea and secretly pursuing their own nuclear weapons.

What was the "Second Korean War"?

The "Second Korean War" was not a war in the formal sense. It did not result in millions of casualties like the 1950–1953 Korean War. Instead, it was a significant uptick in North Korean aggressiveness and violence on and around the Korean Peninsula in the late 1960s.

After the Korean War, North Korean leader Kim Il Sung dedicated much of the rest of the 1950s to eliminating internal rivals and consolidating his power and getting the economy going again. In the trade-off between "guns" (military spending) and "butter" (domestic spending), the mid- to late 1950s was a time of focus on the "butter." However, that focus would not last for long because Kim renewed a military build-up in the 1960s. By the latter part of the decade, Kim grew more aggressive and seemed prepared to use that military force.

Kim Il Sung's forces never invaded South Korea as they had in 1950, but there was a sharp increase in the number of military clashes along the DMZ in the late 1960s against both American and South Korean soldiers. One study showed forty-two military incidents in 1965, against 286 in the first half of 1967. The sudden spike led the Pentagon to call Korea a hostile fire zone again.[11]

In January 1968, North Korea sent commandos to Seoul to try to assassinate South Korean President Park Chung-hee in what became known as the Blue House raid. The Blue House is the South Korea's version of the White House, and the North Korean commandos came stunningly close to breaching the presidential residence and office.

When South Korea's enhanced security measures along the DMZ after the Blue House raid made North Korean land incursions more difficult, the North Koreans came by sea. In October 1968, North Korea again attempted to overthrow the South Korean president, covertly inserting into South Korea over a hundred commandos. They attempted to foment revolution against the increasingly authoritarian South Korean leader. They failed. In December 1969, North Korean intelligence agents hijacked a South Korean civilian airliner and flew it into North Korea. Pyongyang later released some but not all of the victims.

North Korea's violence was also directed at American forces. Two days after the Blue House raid, North Korea attacked an American intelligence-gathering ship operating in international waters, killing one American sailor and capturing sixty-seven others along with the American vessel. North Korea held the sailors as prisoners for a year, and it still retains the vessel, the *USS Pueblo*. North Korea uses the American spy ship today as a museum and propaganda piece, denouncing "American imperialism." In April 1969, North Korea also shot down an unarmed American reconnaissance plane, killing thirty-one.[12]

North Korea's socialist allies worried that Pyongyang actions could trigger full-scale war. The Soviets criticized North Korea's aggressiveness, showing again that Moscow was not controlling Pyongyang.[13] But the conflict did not escalate to general war, and North Korea's aggressiveness moderated. Aggressive and violent North Korean actions continued on land, in the air, and on the sea, but they did not return to the late 1960s levels. In the 1970s, North Korea shifted to encouraging the United States' military withdrawal from South Korea, which appeared to have a reasonable chance of success when the United States withdrew from Vietnam and American presidents suggested or pledged something similar in Korea.

What was South Korea's Yushin Constitution (and North Korea's response)?

In 1972, South Korean President Park Chung-hee suspended the constitution and instituted a new one called the Yushin Constitution. It was a turn toward increasing authoritarianism in South Korea, and Kim Il Sung quickly followed suit with his own new constitution that also augmented the North Korean leader's formal powers. Park's move was the more notable development in a certain sense as South Korea had shifted from low-quality democracy to fully fledged authoritarianism. North Korea was still more repressive than South Korea, but the change was greater in Seoul. Kim's constitutional change codified the personal power that he had continued to amass since his purging rivals and factionalists in the 1950s.

Park's Yushin Constitution should be placed in the context of the Republic of Korea's brief political history at the time. This is not to excuse Park's action but to more fully understand it. From the founding of the ROK in 1948 until 1960, Syngman Rhee ran South Korea. He adjusted electoral rules and term limits to keep himself in power longer. He harassed and blocked political opponents to secure his hold on power while retaining a democratic facade, in part, to assuage the demands of the Americans. Amid allegations of electoral fraud, protest, and violence, Rhee finally resigned in 1960 and fled to the United States, where he died five years later. A weak parliamentary system briefly followed, but General Park Chung-hee orchestrated a successful coup in May 1961.

General Park could claim in 1961 that he sought to restore political stability to South Korea amid a continuing North Korean threat to pave the way for elections. Under American pressure to make the promises of elections a reality, Park's military government held elections in 1963. Park narrowly won, and he won again four years later, in 1967. During Park's second term, South Korea's main opposition party in the National Assembly put forward a constitutional amendment to limit the president to two terms. Park's party dominated the legislature and was not ready to endorse this provision, but protests in the streets drove them to limit the president to three consecutive terms. A nationwide referendum in 1969 cemented the presidential term limit.

Park ran for his third term as president in 1971 and won again. Upon taking office for his third term, which the constitution now held must be his last, Park decided to change the rules. He declared martial law and ten months later dismissed the National Assembly, suspended the constitution, and instituted the new Yushin Constitution by his own decree. The authoritarian move expanded Park's ability to stay in power indefinitely and greatly increased his presidential powers. Park remained in office until his 1979 assassination by his close aide and spy chief, Kim Jae-kyu.

Shortly after Park's Yushin Constitution, Kim Il Sung showed that he would not be outdone. Although Kim's government criticized Park's increasing authoritarianism, it had little moral legitimacy to cast aspersions. Kim's regime had been more repressive than Park's since the early years of the DPRK, and North Korea's 1972 constitution offered Kim the opportunity to lay out what was already clear: Kim's paramount position in

North Korean politics. North Korea's 1972 constitution established a new position for Kim Il Sung—president. He was no longer the premier running the government or the top leader of the Korean Workers' Party among a group of senior party officials. Now Kim was constitutionally and institutionally superior to the party. It was not the Communist Party's regime but Kim's regime.

As Kim Il Sung moved to designate a successor, a provision not detailed in the constitution, Kim did not "keep it all in the party" but opted instead to "keep it in the family." The Kim bloodline and Kim Il Sung's personal decision would be more important than any party decision in naming North Korea's next leader—or any of the other most significant decisions of state.

What was the 1972 North-South Joint Communique?

In 1972, North Korean and South Korean representatives met for the first time. They produced an agreement, or communique, on July 4, 1972 called "The July 4 North-South Joint Communique."[14] The two states agreed that Koreans, not foreigners, should determine the future of the Korean Peninsula, and that they would work together toward unification. The historic agreement floundered in the implementation stage because the two sides were far apart in practice on how to achieve this general ambition.

A changing international environment prompted Seoul and Pyongyang to come together to issue the Joint Communique. Both worried about abandonment by their superpower patrons and increasingly questioned whether the superpowers would look out for Korean interests. In February 1972, President Richard Nixon made the first trip by an American president to China, where he met with Chinese leader Mao Zedong to discuss establishing diplomatic relations. The preparatory meetings between Secretary of State Henry Kissinger and Chinese Premier Zhou Enlai were held in secret and without prior American or Chinese consultation with their allies, creating anxiety in Seoul and Pyongyang that the superpowers might negotiate away their interests in their quest to improve the broader relationship.[15]

The United States and the Soviet Union were also in the midst of détente, which relaxed tensions between the Cold War adversaries.[16] Seoul and Pyongyang were uncertain how Washington and Moscow might sacrifice Korean interests to improve relations with the other superpower. On top of these great-power politics, the United States also appeared to be disengaging militarily from Asia. The United States was trying to extract itself from the long and bloody war in Vietnam. South Vietnam worried that an American military withdrawal would mean the end of their country, which turned out to be correct a few years later, and South Korea did not want to fall into the same situation. In 1969, President Nixon said that America's Asian allies, naming South Vietnam and South Korea, needed to provide more for their own defense,[17] and Nixon withdrew one third of the American troops in South Korea in 1971.[18] In this context, the two Koreas wanted to take their future into their own hands.

Beyond this general commitment that Koreans should be in charge of their own destiny, the two sides searched for specific areas to advance this objective. The two Koreas promised to stop slandering each other, encouraged cultural exchanges and dialogue, and established a military hotline between the two sides to reduce the prospects of miscalculation and the escalation of conflict. The two Koreas held three rounds of government-to-government talks after the Joint Communique to advance inter-Korean reconciliation, but they had far different objectives.

South Korea wanted to start with easy areas of cooperation such as family reunions and cultural exchanges, while North Korea wanted to address the hard issues of security and the political organization of a unified Korean state. Neither was completely forthright about its intentions; each continued to want to preserve its independence and to seek advantage over its rival. When the South Korean military government tried in 1973 to kill a prominent South Korean opposition figure and activist, Kim Dae-jung, North Korea used the event as pretext to call off the negotiations. The Joint Communique would remain an important historical document and basis for later inter-Korean efforts, but it did not advance inter-Korean cooperation to meet the document's lofty ambitions in the 1970s.

Did North Korea try to assassinate South Korean leaders?

Yes. North Korean government operatives attempted to assassinate South Korean presidents on at least two occasions. They never succeeded, but they came close and killed large numbers of South Korean cabinet members, among others, in the course of these efforts. North Korean assassins have contracted or conducted hits on various Koreans, including South Korean officials and high-level North Korean defectors. A North Korean sympathizer also attempted to assassinate the South Korean president in 1974 and inadvertently killed the South Korean first lady instead, but the North Korean government has attempted directly to kill the South Korean president on two known occasions.

In 1968, North Korea sent a team of commandos into South Korea. In a brazen effort to kill President Park Chung-hee at the South Korean presidential office and residence, the Blue House, the North Korean team came perilously close to doing so. They were spotted by a group of South Korean civilians in the mountains behind the Blue House, but surprisingly, the North Korean commando leader let the young hikers go. They informed South Korean police, triggering a massive search for the North Korean commandos that would leave scores of

South Koreans dead. The whole commando team was killed or committed suicide, but not before coming within a hundred yards of the Blue House.

In 1983, the North Koreans tried again. They attempted to kill another South Korean general who had come to power in a coup to assume the presidency, Chun Doo-hwan, in an apparent bid to foment chaos and revolution in South Korea. Instead of striking at the South Korean president at his heavily-defended office and residence, the North Koreans this time struck while Chun was traveling abroad.

Chun was supposed to lay a wreath at a cemetery in Rangoon, Burma, but his motorcade was late. A bomb planted by North Korean operatives detonated, killing seventeen South Koreans. Included among the dead were four South Korean cabinet ministers and two senior presidential aides who were awaiting the president's arrival. Declassified CIA reports from the time show clear evidence of North Korean involvement, including the use of known North Korean military equipment and North Korean operatives caught trying to escape the country by ship.[19]

Since South Korea's democratization in the late 1980s, there have not been any publicized North Korean efforts to assassinate South Korean presidents. The political effort to sow social discord in South Korea through these assassinations applied more during the South Korean authoritarian period. Assassinating a democratic leader causes tremendous shock, horror, and pain for the victim's family and country. But democratic processes ensure that another democratic leader will legally take the helm to continue the republic. The assassination of a South Korean military leader who had unconstitutionally seized power could usher in uncertainty or political chaos, because the country lacks a clear mechanism to establish a successor government. Contemporary South Korean political leaders require security, but the likelihood of another North Korean hit on a South Korean president appears increasingly remote.

Who led South Korea during the democracy movement and consolidation?

During South Korea's democratization movement, the country was in the midst of a process toward democracy. Consequently, military leaders continued to rule the government, controlled the coercive institutions of the police and military, and even retained significant influence with the largest business conglomerates that dominated the economy. At the same time, opposition leaders enjoyed growing support from the people, as popular protest swelled.

Calls for more representative democracy and even social protest date back much earlier in Korea than the 1980s, but the massive protests that culminated in South Korean democratization were most poignant during this decade. After Park Chung-hee's 1979 assassination and a brief interregnum, General Chun Doo-hwan seized power in 1980. He remained president until 1988. Chun responded to the democracy movement with a heavy hand. In 1980, he cracked down on protesters in the southwest Korean city of Gwangju. The bloody persecution furthered the cause of the pro-democracy movement as protest grew larger and harder to ignore.

In 1987, Chun allowed open elections. It was not the first time a South Korean military leader had allowed democratic elections, and past elections have been used as a facade to legitimize continued authoritarian rule. Thus it was not a foregone conclusion that democracy would stick after 1987. But it did.

South Korea elected a conservative with ties to the military regime in 1987, Roh Tae-woo. Roh ran against "the three Kims," referring to Kim Dae-jung, Kim Young-sam, and Kim Jong-pil, who split the opposition vote between them and allowed General Chun's favored successor to win. Five years later, in 1992, the South Korean electorate again returned a conservative to the Blue House, this time a former dissident who was critical of the authoritarian regime, but still precluding a transfer of power to the other side of the political spectrum.

South Korea would see the first transfer of presidential power from the conservative to the progressive camp in 1997, when the country elected Kim Dae-jung. Political scientists define democratic consolidation differently, but the peaceful transfer of power in competitive elections is a critical test of a democracy's strength. One can say South Korea democratized in the 1980s, and it consolidated this democracy in the 1990s.

How did South Korea democratize?

South Korea democratized through a process of grass-roots popular mobilization against the ruling military government. Democratization is a complex phenomenon in any country and the most studied concept in the discipline of comparative politics. As such, many scholars debate the importance of additional considerations above and beyond this basic rubric. The nature of South Korea's rapidly expanding economy and deep integration into the global economy created foreign pressure to liberalize the political system. Likewise, Seoul's ally, the United States, had long advocated improved human rights and democratic standards, but this pressure did not reach a peak with South Korea's actual movement toward representative government.

A variety of domestic social and economic factors and international influences affect this political process, but it is difficult to see how the South Korean military government could have decided to allow elections and relinquish control without the massive and sustained outpouring of South Koreans, including college students and newly unified unions, which organized strikes around the country. Focused on ensuring a smooth 1988 Seoul Summer Olympics and confident that his successor could win a democratic poll, General Chun acquiesced. The opposition split the vote, allowing Chun's preferred candidate, Roh Tae-woo, to win a plurality. Nevertheless, South Korea did not return to military government as its democracy matured into the 1990s and beyond.

What was Nordpolitik?

Nordpolitik was South Korea's effort in the waning years of the Cold War to reach out to the socialist world, including North Korea. It was named after West Germany's Ostpolitik policy that sought to reach out to East Germany, but the Korean variant was not exclusively a national unification effort. It was a broader outreach to Moscow and Beijing first that had important indirect impacts on the inter-Korean relationship. Though the idea preceded South Korean President Roh Tae-woo, Roh adopted Nordpolitik as a central pillar of his foreign policy upon his inauguration in 1988.[20]

North Korea and South Korea used much of the Cold War to court foreign powers to support and recognize their government instead of the other Korea. North Korea counted the Soviet Union and China, as the most significant socialist states in the international system, as firmly on their side. Despite decades of very real difficulties in Pyongyang's relations with the communist giants, the Kim regime did not need to worry that Moscow or Beijing would abandon ship and cozy up with its American-backed nemesis in South Korea. Likewise, South Korea, as an American treaty ally, counted itself as firmly within the US orbit.

As the Cold War came to an end, this neat division of patrons started to shift—decidedly in Seoul's favor. Moscow and Beijing saw South Korea's tremendous economic expansion precisely as North Korea declined as an attractive trade and investment partner. The Soviet Union faced increasing economic difficulties at home in the 1980s, even as it increased its aid to an ungrateful North Korea to keep its socialist partner afloat. China used the 1980s and beyond to shift away from the ideological roots of the Mao era as it reformed its socialist economy with more capitalistic influences. Moscow and Beijing grew more receptive to Seoul's outreach as Pyongyang grew more isolated internationally. Moscow established diplomatic relations with Seoul in 1990, and Beijing did so in 1992, over grave North Korean objections.

The implications of Roh's Nordpolitik foreign policy extended beyond the Korean Peninsula. The United States led a boycott of the 1980 Moscow Olympics, and the Soviet Union did the same for the 1984 Los Angeles games. Seoul's hosting the 1988 Olympics was its time to shine on the international stage and showcase its tremendous economic and even democratic advances. Roh did not want to see another boycott, and his outreach to the socialist countries helped ensure a well-attended Olympics. However, even this development was wrapped up in inter-Korean politics. Pyongyang urged a boycott of the Seoul games after it failed in a long negotiating effort to win cohosting rights. Pyongyang's socialist allies did not take up the cause and went to Seoul over Pyongyang's wishes.

Roh utilized North Korea's increasing international isolation as the Cold War came to an end to engage Pyongyang from a position of strength. The two Koreas negotiated two important documents, which came into force in 1992: the Agreement on Reconciliation, Nonaggression, and Exchanges and Cooperation (also known as "the Basic Agreement), and the Joint Declaration of the Denuclearization of the Korean Peninsula. Implementing both agreements faced difficulties given the ambitious commitments to improving relations, advancing peace, and denuclearizing the Korean Peninsula.[21] However, Nordpolitik helped create the conditions in which the two sides could at least articulate a shared vision of peaceful coexistence and unification.

Why were the 1988 Seoul Olympic Games important?

The 1988 Summer Olympics were Seoul's opportunity to show the world the advances it had made, bask in the limelight of decades-in-the-making economic and domestic political achievements, and demonstrate that it had won the inter-Korean competition for legitimacy. By 1988, South Korea had a thriving economy with world-class brands exported to every continent. Its citizens enjoyed the middle-class existence of an industrialized country, which contrasted with its own history just a few decades earlier as a poor agricultural state in need of foreign support and aid to develop. Coming off a decade of democratization protests, Seoul could point to its 1987 presidential elections as a turning point toward genuine democratization that would later be shown to stick. South Koreans had much to be proud of, and the Olympics brought the world—and its TV cameras—to the capital to document it.

It was significant that the International Olympic Committee (IOC) selected Seoul, not Pyongyang, to host the games. The IOC announced its decision to accept Seoul's bid for the 1988 Summer Olympics in 1981. Two months after the IOC announcement, Seoul also won the bid to host the 1986 Asian Games.[22] Kim Il Sung called on North Korea's socialist allies to boycott the Seoul Olympics, to no avail. In 1985, Kim proposed equal cohosting of the 1988 Olympics with half of the events in South Korea and half in North Korea. The IOC, North Korea, and South Korea negotiated the matter in 1986 and 1987 but could not reach agreement.

In November 1987, North Korean intelligence agents bombed Korean Airlines flight 858, killing 115 people. A captured North Korean agent involved in the bombing admitted that North Korea had sought to discredit the Seoul Olympics with the terrorist attack. Nevertheless, within two months, Kim Il Sung called for renewed inter-Korean discussions on cohosting the games, and Seoul agreed. However, Kim would not accept a formulation short of equal cohosting, which Roh was not prepared to give. South Korea hosted a successful Olympics, and North Korea stood alone in its boycott.

Pyongyang followed up with its own international event, spending billions to host the World Festival of Youth and Students in 1989. The event paled in comparison to the prestige and international draw of the Olympics. The 1988 Seoul Olympics demonstrated to the world the advances of South Korea eclipsed those of North Korea by a wide margin.

3

POST–COLD WAR

How did the Soviet collapse affect Korea?

The collapse of the Soviet Union in 1991 profoundly affected global politics, including for the Korean Peninsula. The Soviet Union had deep ties with North Korea that spanned the course of North Korea's history as a state. Moscow was Pyongyang's primary security backer and source of economic aid, and the Soviet collapse removed these basic supports for the North Korean government and threatened the regime's basic ability to survive.

An array of Soviet satellite states in Europe, dependent on the Soviet Union in ways roughly similar to North Korea, collapsed in the 1990s. Some made peaceful transitions to democracy, such as the Czech Republic, or peacefully unified as democratic states, such as East and West Germany. Others saw the violent overthrow and execution of communist dictators, such as Romania's Nicolae Ceausescu. North Korea's leaders did not intend to let their regime follow suit.

On the security front, Pyongyang faced a dilemma. The great-power victors in World War II that defeated Japan in 1945 divided the Korean Peninsula into two spheres—North and South. From its inception, North Korea relied on the Soviet Union as its great-power security backer, just as South Korea depended on the United States for the same. Although the

North Koreans would take great pains throughout the Cold War to argue that they were self-sufficient, they ultimately relied on either Beijing or Moscow at various points in their history for critical security and economic inputs. In September 1990, the Soviets established diplomatic relations with South Korea over North Korea's objections, just fifteen months before the Soviet Union disintegrated. The Soviet Union collapsed but the United States did not, creating a security imbalance between the competing Korean governments. South Korea could still rely on the United States as a treaty ally with the most formidable military on the planet, while North Korea increasingly stood alone.

North Korea had long been wary of foreign supporters and had sought to build its own military that could provide for the national defense even in the event of superpower abandonment. It built a large and capable military force, forward deployed along the border with South Korea called the Demilitarized Zone (DMZ). It could inflict serious harm on South Korea, destroy its capital with artillery fire, and at least claim parity with South Korean military capabilities. However, North Korea was no match for the US military, and they knew it. The 1991 Persian Gulf War, when the United States quickly forced Saddam Hussein's Iraqi armed forces to retreat from the invasion of neighboring Kuwait, displaying the far superior US military technology, worried the North Koreans. If the Americans could quickly defeat the large standing army of Saddam Hussein, what would stop them from doing the same in North Korea?

The North Koreans had been exploring nuclear technology for decades. Starting in the 1950s, the North Koreans had claimed they wanted to harness the peaceful benefits of nuclear energy, but even North Korea's closest socialist allies in the 1960s and 1970s viewed its intentions with suspicion. North Korea wanted nuclear weapons. However, they did not make the fateful decision to cross the line toward weaponizing their nuclear technology until the Soviet Union was collapsing.

North Korea attempted to hide its nuclear weapons program but faltered. The Soviet collapse prompted a North Korean security crisis, and North Korea sought to replace its now-defunct great-power supporter with the world's most powerful weapons to deter their main security concern: the United States.

On the economic front, Pyongyang faced an equally daunting challenge. Despite Moscow's increasing economic woes, the Soviet Union actually increased its aid to North Korea throughout the mid-1980s. South Korea's rapid economic expansion was leaving North Korea in the dust, and South Korea's military government at the time leveraged that economic advantage to invest heavily in more advanced military capabilities. The Soviets sought to keep the North Koreans somewhat competitive on the peninsula while simultaneously restraining North Korea from developing nuclear weapons. Aid and concessionary terms of trade were Moscow's tools to try to maintain influence in Pyongyang.

Moscow's aid came crashing down in 1991, when the Soviet Union vanished from the map and was replaced by Russia. Just a year earlier the Soviet Union had been North Korea's top trading partner by a wide margin. Bilateral trade volume stood at over $2.5 billion in 1990—five times more than the total trade volume of North Korea's second most important trade partner at the time, China. In 1991, Russian-DPRK trade dwindled to just $365 million, and other trade partners did not fill in to make up the difference.[1] North Korea–Russia relations hit a new low, and Kim claimed that he did not need to repay the country's Soviet debt obligations to the successor Russian government. Moscow suspended its nuclear assistance to Pyongyang.[2] Moscow's oil shipments to North Korea dropped from 410,000 metric tons in 1990 to 100,000 metric tons in 1991,[3] reducing Kim's industrial and military potential. Russian and Chinese arms shipments to North Korea shrank from over $2 billion in 1987–1989 to just over 3 percent of that value—$65–70 million—in 1992–1994.[4]

Pyongyang had enjoyed important economic inputs from its aid and concessionary trade with Moscow. For example, energy imports fueled North Korean industry. Without this energy supply, inefficient North Korean factories shuttered, and blackouts became increasingly common. A satellite photo of the Korean Peninsula at night famously showed the southern half electrified and the northern half literally in the dark. Amid a severe energy crunch in the 1990s, North Korea, a mountainous country with little arable land, shifted from an economy dominated by industry to one dominated by agriculture. The Soviet collapse was not the only factor, but coupled with poor policy choices in Pyongyang, North Korea's difficult security and economic situation became dire.

How did China modify its Korea policy after the Cold War?

In August 1992, the Chinese Communist Party established diplomatic relations with the Republic of Korea—North Korea's rival in the south. Pyongyang saw it as nothing short of an act of betrayal. For decades, Seoul and Pyongyang had each struggled to present itself as the only legitimate Korean government, rightfully responsible for ruling the entire Korean Peninsula. Each actively sought to run up the score by urging third countries to establish diplomatic relations with it and thereby officially recognize one Korean government as the exclusive representative of the Korean nation. China was the fellow communist government that came to North Korea's aid in the Korean War. The eldest son of the revolutionary Chinese leader Mao Zedong had died in the war, and the two countries had feigned something of a special relationship since their founding. Now, not even China was fully in North Korea's court.

However, the China–North Korea relationship had been fraught from the beginning. The end of the US-Soviet superpower standoff did not prompt China's move to recognize South Korea, and the China–North Korea relationship would actually become more important in the decades to come. Chinese Communist Party chairman Mao Zedong was never enthusiastic about entering the Korean War, and North Korean leader Kim Il Sung likewise sought to minimize and control China's military intervention. After the war, Kim demanded the withdrawal of Chinese forces from North Korean territory, and the history of the two countries' bilateral relations is replete with evidence of a strained relationship. China had become more pragmatic and less ideological since beginning economic reform in the late 1970s, and fraternal communist links only went so far.

China's diplomatic recognition of the Republic of Korea had more to do with South Korea's own tremendous economic success, especially relative to North Korea's moribund economy, than with the end of the US-Soviet confrontation. South Korea started to overtake North Korea economically in the 1970s, but the gap widened dramatically and irreversibly in the 1980s. China–South Korea trade eclipsed China–North Korea trade in the 1980s as Beijing tried to convince Pyongyang to reform its economy as China had done.[5] China's decision to establish diplomatic relations with South Korea came amid an unmistakable realization that South Korea had become substantially more significant in economic terms than its northern neighbor.

The China–North Korea relationship soured quickly and remained at a low ebb through much of the 1990s, but China became increasingly central to North Korea's foreign policy and external trade in the 2000s, as the DPRK increasingly isolated itself. China–North Korea bilateral trade dropped between 1993 and 1996 but then rebounded. Bilateral trade initially decreased, as China demanded a market-oriented trading relationship and ceased to provide "friendship prices" based on a political rather than economic logic. However, as North Korea sank into a famine that had become increasingly apparent by 1996 and North Korea watchers increasingly discussed the possibility of the country's imminent collapse,

Beijing responded by throwing Pyongyang a lifeline with concessionary trade and aid.

Beijing's decision in 1996 to reverse its demand that North Korea be treated as a normal state, where business logic drives trade and investment decisions and humanitarian considerations determine aid, in favor of the old model of decisions based on more purely political motives, underlines the limits of China's influence with North Korea. China has repeatedly urged North Korea to follow its economic reform model and refrain from pursuing nuclear weapons, but its threats to cut off the North Koreans often ring hollow. China does not want instability on its border, especially from a nuclear-armed country, and North Korea can use its weakness as an asset. By suggesting that its regime could fall apart or lash out against what it describes as US pressure, Pyongyang has maintained a subsistence level of Chinese support. In the post–Cold War era, North Korea and China frequently saw things in a very different light, but strategic interests kept Beijing supporting Pyongyang in important but limited ways.

What happened when North Korean leader Kim Il Sung died?

When North Korean founder Kim Il Sung died in 1994, there was an outpouring of public demonstrations of grief by North Koreans. Western media portrayed the crying masses as a show orchestrated by the North Korean regime. There was likely some of that, but it appears that some of the grief may have been genuine. Gauging individuals' unspoken motives and inner feelings is always difficult, and the North Korean people certainly had a strong self-interest in publicly reaffirming their loyalty to the Kim regime through expressions of sorrow. However, North Korean defectors living in the south who are deeply critical of the Kim regime today often still speak positively about Kim Il Sung. Based on a select telling of history based on grains of truth, the North Koreans seemed to have genuine affection for their first leader.

In the North Korean telling of events, Kim Il Sung established the Korean Peoples' Army, the Korean Workers' Party, and then the North Korean state. He is their George Washington figure on steroids. He fought the brutal Japanese colonization of Korea, which actively sought to suppress Korean national identity, and emphasized an extreme Korean nationalism as a guiding principle of his rule after Japan's defeat in World War II and withdrawal from Korea. Kim Il Sung fought the Korean War to unify the Korean nation; the American imperialist intervention blocked his ambition. He rebuilt the North Korean economy from the rubble of three years of war into one that outpaced South Korean economic growth rates for the first two decades of their mutual existence as states. Though it would not be completely fair, a North Korean critical of his or her country's state of affairs could blame Kim Jong Il and his successor for ruining what Kim Il Sung had started.

Kim Il Sung first selected his eldest son, Kim Jong Il, as his successor in the 1970s. He formally announced his decision at the Sixth Party Congress in 1980, and Kim Il Sung gradually shifted roles and responsibilities to his son throughout the decade. In 1992, Kim Il Sung told a Western journalist that his son ran the country.[6] Kim Il Sung was nominally the leader of North Korea when he died in 1994 at age eighty-two and retained important ceremonial roles, including receiving former US president Jimmy Carter in the midst of a nuclear crisis, but his death did not mark a sudden change or stimulate a succession crisis. Kim Jong Il continued to run the country.

Who was North Korean leader Kim Jong Il?

Kim Jong Il was the second leader of North Korea and the eldest son of the country's founder, Kim Il Sung. Unlike his father, who came from humble beginnings and made a name from himself by leading a small band of guerilla fighters against the Japanese colonialists, Kim Jong Il grew up in privilege. He owed his position to his bloodline rather than his own actions. Kim Il Sung cut his teeth as a military leader, while Kim Jong Il was passionate about cultural projects, especially film. In contrast to his charismatic father who tried to stay above the fray and gave general policy guidance, Kim Jong Il was an introvert and micromanaged governmental process. Kim Jong Il became North Korea's leader exclusively because of his role as his father's son, so it is important to consider him against North Korea's own point of reference in comparison to his larger than life father.

Kim Jong Il was groomed as successor starting in the 1970s, announced as the heir designate in 1980, and gradually took on more roles as the regime's top leader over the course of the decade. When Kim Jong Il formally became the leader of North Korea upon his father's death in 1994, his country was facing its most extreme security and economic crisis since the Korean War. In the early 1990s, Kim Jong Il, along with his ailing father, oversaw a nuclear crisis with the world's sole remaining superpower, the United States, that raised the credible risk of war. He also was at the helm as North Korea sank into famine later that decade.

North Korea's security and economic crises had their roots deep in the Kim Il Sung era, but Kim Jong Il also had an important role and had the paramount responsibility to respond to both crises. Fairly or not, Kim Il Sung became associated internally with North Korea's perceived rise, while Kim Jong Il oversaw the country's steep decline. Even North Korean defectors deeply critical of the North Korean government often hold Kim Il Sung in high regard and blame Kim Jong Il for failures. The third North Korean leader, the youngest Kim, has distanced himself from his unpopular late father and seeks to model himself on his revered grandfather.

All three Kims leading North Korea have utilized brutal repression tactics, including purges, executions, long-term incarcerations of political prisoners, and punishment of family members of those deemed political enemies. Since the 1960s, North Korea has categorized individuals based on their family background into the "core," "wavering," and "hostile" classes. Perceived political loyalty to the Kim family became the critical determinant of social and economic privilege under the Songbun social classification system. The Kim regime rewarded loyalists with prioritized housing and healthcare, educational access for their children, and prestigious jobs in the party, military, or government. The three Kims used many of the same tools to safeguard elite loyalty, repress dissent or potential dissent, and secure their position atop the ruling apparatus. However, Kim Jong Il's personality and ruling style preferences were still markedly different from Kim Il Sung's methods despite ruling the same regime consecutively.

What was the North Korean famine?

The North Korean famine was the greatest tragedy for ordinary North Koreans since the Korean War. The famine reached its zenith in the mid- to late 1990s, and credible estimates are that the famine claimed the lives of six hundred thousand to one million North Koreans.[7]

North Korea has long suffered chronic food shortages, so the famine did not suddenly appear overnight. One sophisticated analysis began by simply asking North Korean defectors when they started having difficulty finding enough food to eat; some respondents recalled that these "lean years" began as early as the late 1980s.[8] However, North Korea is prone to flooding, and particularly heavy rains and flooding in 1995 and 1996 reduced the country's crop and accelerated the shift from chronic malnutrition to full-blown famine. The most extreme deprivation occurred in the 1995–1998 time frame, after which North Korea's food situation and economy started to see improvements.

The North Korean government labeled the famine years "the arduous march." The regime called on its people to provide more for themselves as the state's ability to supply the most basic requirements of life failed. Pyongyang literally tried to "blame it on the rain," arguing that the regime had no control over the weather and that the extreme flooding had reduced agricultural output and prompted famine. However, famines are more complex than simply an insufficient quantity of food. North Korean leaders urged self-sufficiency as a political tenet, which also applied to providing for the nation's food supply. Though as a mountainous country, North Korea has little farmland, its leadership preferred to make herculean efforts to carve farmland out of mountainsides and to engage in the extensive use of chemical fertilizers that threatened soil erosion and exhaustion. Instead of exporting more industrial goods to buy food imports, the regime made a decision to prioritize self-sufficiency.

When North Korea faced food shortages, Kim Jong Il was slow to react. He was hesitant to allow international aid workers to distribute relief. When he did allow aid workers into the country, he heavily restricted their activities.[9] North Korea also actually *decreased* its commercial food imports during the famine as international aid started to flow in. Rather than use the international support to augment domestic food production and increasing or at least keeping constant their food imports, North Korea shifted these economic resources away from food imports to other regime priorities.[10] Government policies therefore put North Korea on the precipice of a food emergency, and misplaced regime priorities exacerbated the crisis into a full-scale famine.

North Korea's famine tremendously affected North Korean society and its economy. Although members of the political elite and ordinary North Koreans alike suffered food shortages, they did not do so equally. The state-controlled food distribution prioritized the Pyongyang-based elite and certain sectoral workers, including the military. Farmers could siphon off portions of their production more easily, thus city dwellers outside Pyongyang and vulnerable groups, such as children, the elderly, and the infirm, were at the most risk. Many people died waiting for the regime to deliver on its promises of resuming the delivery of food; others coped by crossing into China or engaging in black market trade, or both. Most North Korean defectors crossing into China were women. North Korean women were trafficked for sexual exploitation by Chinese men or sold to Chinese husbands, who sought to keep their "investments" from escaping and often treated them accordingly. This compounded the human tragedy of the North Korean famine. There were also reports of increases in prostitution inside North Korea, as desperate people struggled to survive and provide for their families.

Others, also often women, sought to make money to provide for themselves and their families by engaging in illegal petty trade. The state's distribution network was inefficient and led to much spoilage of foodstuffs, compounding an already bleak situation. Black markets helped distribute goods more efficiently by connecting consumers and producers but ran afoul of North Korea's ideological orthodoxy that the state would provide for the people in line with socialist principles. The regime intermittently cracked down on black markets, which gradually inched toward becoming legal markets guided by a peculiar set of state regulations. Nevertheless, North Korea's famine and the response by desperate people to survive stimulated a bottom-up change in the North Korean economy that the regime eventually recognized could not be fully reversed. It set the stage for additional North Korean economic reforms years later.

What is North Korea's military-first ideology?

North Korea's military-first ideology was introduced in the mid-1990s to augment the guiding political philosophy of *Juche*. As North Korean founder Kim Il Sung consolidated his power internally in the 1950s, he gave a major speech outlining an ideology that would guide his regime. *Juche*, which is often translated as "self-reliance," is a malleable concept that emphasizes Korean nationalism over reliance on foreign powers or methods. Kim distinguished the North Korean version of Marxism-Leninism from the Soviet or Chinese meaning, ushering in decades of vague references to "Korean-style socialism." *Juche* applied to all walks of life and politics. For example, North Korea's foreign and security policy sought to maximize its freedom of movement in foreign affairs by avoiding dependence on any single foreign backer, which led Kim Il Sung to maneuver between the Soviets and the Chinese for support during the Sino-Soviet split. With *Juche* and Korean nationalism as its guide, North Korea has repeatedly criticized South Korea for allowing foreign forces (US troops) to permanently station on Korean soil. Pyongyang calls this an affront to sovereignty and raises this point in particular whenever American service personnel stationed in South Korea commit crimes against Koreans. Likewise, *Juche* agriculture involves trying to grow the country's own food supply instead of selling North Korean industrial outputs and buying agricultural products from abroad.

After Kim Il Sung's death, in 1994, his eldest son and successor Kim Jong Il eventually added another ideological precept called "military first." Kim Jong Il did not eliminate *Juche* but augmented it with the military-first policy, or military-first ideology. North Korea had long prioritized the military sector in resource allocation, and the military-first policy, in part, reinforced that idea. More significantly, Kim Jong Il raised the status and role of the military as an institution to help him run the country. In 1998, Kim Jong Il established the National Defense Commission and made himself the chairman. In addition to being the general secretary of the Korean Workers' Party, Kim now had another hat. He revised the constitution to make the main institutions of the party, military, and government report to him directly instead of through a comprehensive party institution, as under Kim Il Sung.

Kim Jong Il faced crisis, and he sought greater technocratic competence, not just ideological correctness, to get through the particularly difficult period in North Korean history. He also seemed to want to make sure to keep the military placated and on his side to avoid the risk of a coup that could unseat him. The North Korean military was a hierarchal institution that could help Kim with the "emergency management" necessary to traverse the crisis. After Kim Jong Il's death, his son and successor would effectively end these emergency-management procedures in favor of Kim Il Sung's "normal" operations of state that relied on a comprehensive Korean Workers' Party to guide government and military policy under his ultimate direction.

Who was South Korean President Kim Dae-jung?

Kim Dae-jung was a progressive South Korean politician and dissident who rose to become South Korea's president a decade after democratization. Following the establishment of the Republic of Korea in 1948, South Korea's first president, Syngman Rhee, ruled over what can most charitably be called a "low-quality democracy." Rhee was elected to office but only after abuses of power, including electoral manipulation, extrajudicial imprisonments and executions, and other human rights abuses incompatible with democratic norms. South Korean general Park Chung-hee orchestrated a coup in 1961, and he became president two years later. His long-time aide and spy chief assassinated him in office in 1979.

Kim Dae-jung purposed himself as an opponent to this system of the authoritarian government and championed democratization. He spoke out against the increasingly authoritarian policies of South Korean dictator Park Chung-hee after Park declared martial law. Kim was the target of at least five assassination attempts, including one in which South Korean intelligence operatives kidnapped him, and the United States had to intervene with its ally to demand his release. In 2000, the Nobel Committee awarded Kim Dae-jung the Nobel Peace Prize.

South Korea's democratization movement accelerated in the 1980s, culminating in a transition to democracy by the end of the decade. Kim failed to win the presidency in early attempts, but the South Korean people elected him president in 1997. President Kim Dae-jung advocated engagement with North Korea that sought to transform decades of confrontation into peaceful coexistence—a policy he termed the Sunshine Policy. Kim died in 2009 but remains popular among South Korean progressives and unpopular among South Korean conservatives; the two sides remain sharply divided on North Korea policy.

What was the Sunshine Policy?

The Sunshine Policy was South Korean president Kim Dae-jung's (1998–2003) North Korea engagement policy. The Sunshine Policy took its name from the Aesop's fable in which the warm sun and cold wind compete to encourage a man to remove his coat; like Aesop, Kim believed that warmth would prevail. He encouraged generous inter-Korean economic projects and aid, cultural exchanges, reunions of families separated for decades by the division of the Korean nation, and carried out the first inter-Korean summit in 2000. Kim hoped to reduce tensions and increase North Korean reliance on the South economically to gradually transform the relationship from one dominated by confrontation to one that could produce peace and eventually allow for the unification of the Korean nation.

Sunshine Policy supporters argued this was a long-term effort. Decades-old confrontation would not end overnight as they sought a fundamental transformation in the inter-Korean relationship. They counted the number of government-to-government and people-to-people exchanges, trade volume, and amount of humanitarian assistance as barometers of success, given the difficulty in quantifying the progress of such a long-term project. South Korean presidents are limited constitutionally to a single, five-year term, but Kim's successor, Roh Moo-hyun, sought to continue the policy under another name.

Kim's Sunshine Policy was controversial in South Korea. South Korean conservatives derided the approach as naïve and dangerous. They charged that South Korea got nothing in return for its expensive investments in the North as Pyongyang continued to develop nuclear weapons and keep a formidable military forward deployed along the DMZ. South Korea's "give aways" to the North helped keep the country afloat at the precise moment that it suffered the greatest challenges and may otherwise have collapsed, Kim's critics charged. Later revelations that Kim Dae-jung's government paid North Korea a half billion dollars to secure the first inter-Korean summit further soured South Korean public opinion on the unconditional engagement approach.

South Korean conservatives also argued the Sunshine Policy jeopardized the US–South Korea alliance that was the foundation of South Korea's defense against the North. After the presidential transition in the United States from Bill Clinton to George W. Bush in 2000, the new American administration ordered a review of US North Korea policy. While the Bush administration initially settled on something similar to its predecessor's approach, it shifted gears after the terrorist attacks on the United States on September 11, 2001. Hard-line approaches came to dominate, including on North Korea policy, and Kim Dae-jung and George W. Bush clashed over their approaches to North Korea. Instead of affirming alliance solidarity, the two partners found themselves far apart.

South Korea's electorate gave the Sunshine experiment a decade's try but decided in 2007 to elect a conservative president who pledged to reimpose conditionality on South Korean largesse, demanding that North Korea move toward denuclearization before granting greater economic benefits. South Korean conservatives welcomed the end of ten years of progressive rule, while South Korean progressives lamented the undoing of their efforts.

4

NUCLEAR WEAPONS AND US–NORTH KOREA RELATIONS

When did North Korea first pursue nuclear technology?

North Korea first demonstrated interest in nuclear technology in the 1950s. North Korean leader Kim Il Sung likely learned about the power of nuclear weapons in August 1945, along with most of the world, when the United States detonated nuclear weapons over Hiroshima and Nagasaki to precipitate the end of World War II in the Pacific. Kim subsequently focused on consolidating his power at home and unifying Korea by force in the 1950–1953 Korean War, which did not provide a conducive environment to building nuclear power plants for weapons or energy. Nevertheless, in 1952 North Korea established the Atomic Energy Research Institute but did not start to make progress on its nuclear program until its cooperation with Moscow advanced. By 1956, the Soviet ambassador in Pyongyang recorded in his journal, "Kim Il Sung said that Korean scientists have long raised the question to us of getting an opportunity to work in the field of nuclear research."[1] The Soviet ambassador's record suggests this was not the first time the North Koreans had requested such assistance, but it is the first historical record of the request that we have.

Kim Il Sung's request came in the context of the 1950s understanding and norms governing nuclear technology. In 1953, President Dwight Eisenhower delivered his "Atoms for Peace" speech. He warned about the grave dangers of atomic weapons and stressed the need to expedite the "peaceful use of atomic energy."[2] Nuclear technology had civilian purposes related to energy production, medicine, and general scientific research, as well as military purposes related to building weapons. North Korea presented itself early as interested in the peaceful benefits of nuclear technology even while its closest allies remained firmly skeptical of North Korea's peaceful intentions from the beginning.

In 1958, the United States introduced tactical nuclear weapons to South Korea. To try to defend its treaty ally from another North Korean invasion without having to permanently station an even larger American military presence on the peninsula, the United States deployed and controlled lower-yield and shorter-range nuclear weapons that were intended to defend South Korea. North Korea found the move threatening and continued to seek its own nuclear help from its socialist bloc allies.

The Soviets provided North Korea an IRT-2000 research reactor in 1963, and it went operational two years later, as Pyongyang continued to push for more.[3] Foreign nuclear assistance jump-started North Korea's nuclear effort, but the country made significant indigenous strides as well. In the early 1980s, North Korea began construction of its five-megawatt (5MW) reactor at Yongbyon. Although it was based on an obsolete 1950s design for a British nuclear reactor, the 5MW reactor would substantially advance North Korea's ability to develop the necessary inputs for a nuclear weapon.

Did South Korea have a nuclear weapons program too?

South Korea's then military government had pursued nuclear weapons in the 1970s. South Korean dictator Park Chung-hee initiated a secret nuclear weapons program in 1972. North Korea's conventional military was superior to South Korea's force, and Park relied on his American ally fundamentally for

South Korea's national security. But Park increasingly feared that Washington would abandon Seoul in pursuit of its wider global agenda in the 1970s, and he sought nuclear weapons to guarantee national security.

In 1969, President Richard Nixon noted that America's Asian allies would have to do more to provide for their own security. Targeting his remarks mainly at South Vietnam but also naming South Korea, Nixon said that the United States "must avoid the kind of policy that will make countries in Asia so dependent upon us that we are dragged into conflicts such as the one we have in Vietnam." The United States would honor its treaty commitments to defend its allies, especially related to providing a nuclear umbrella against Soviet threats, but, he said, Asian nations must otherwise take more responsibility for providing for their own defense.[4] In the context of the American withdrawal from Vietnam and the collapse of South Vietnam, Park Chung-hee was worried. Nixon's historic trip to China in 1972, which seemed to the Koreans to value great-power priorities over the interests of America's smaller allies, furthered the South Korean fear of abandonment.

Park established South Korea's Agency for Defense Development in 1973 and notably sought nuclear assistance from France, not the United States. He outlined an ambitious schedule, hoping to develop nuclear weapons by the early 1980s.[5] American intelligence learned about Park's secret effort, and Washington intervened to stop it, fearing further nuclear proliferation by other countries. Under American pressure, Park signed the Nuclear Nonproliferation Treaty in 1975, pledging to forgo nuclear weapons, and canceled a nuclear reprocessing agreement with France in 1976, but he still moved ahead with nuclear research.[6]

In the 1976 US presidential election campaign, candidate Jimmy Carter promised to withdraw American troops from South Korea, a move North Korean leader Kim Il Sung welcomed. Within a month of his inauguration in 1977, President Carter sent Park a letter showing his intent to keep his campaign promise. Objecting to Park's human rights abuses, Carter raised the possibility of a complete US military withdrawal and set in place a specific plan to do so the following month. Park was worried and even tried to bribe members of Congress to oppose the plan, sparking a scandal that would be later dubbed "Koreagate." Despite stiff resistance within his own government based on the concern that removing US forces would leave South Korea vulnerable to North Korean invasion, Carter pressed forward. Park finally agreed to scrap his nuclear weapons program in 1979, as Carter ended his planned military withdrawal.[7] For unrelated reasons, Park's close confidant assassinated him later in 1979. Park's successor completely ended South Korea's nuclear program in 1981 amid President Ronald Reagan's robust American military support for South Korea.

Why did North Korea sign the Nuclear Nonproliferation Treaty?

Under strong Soviet pressure, North Korea signed the Nuclear Nonproliferation Treaty (NPT) in 1985, pledging to forgo nuclear weapons. However, North Korea did not let this legal restriction block its pursuit of nuclear weapons.

In 1968, the United States, the Soviet Union, and a variety of other nations reached agreement on the NPT. The treaty would establish a global norm to limit the spread of nuclear weapons and go on to have more signatories than any other treaty outside the United Nations Charter. From the outset, North Korea resisted signing a treaty that would legally prohibit them from pursuing nuclear weapons. The multilateral treaty locked in the five states that had developed nuclear weapons prior to the treaty's negotiation as the five nuclear weapons states. The nuclear weapons states pledged to negotiate "in good faith" their own nuclear disarmament, but the NPT's critics, including North Korea, charged that the arrangement was discriminatory. By allowing the early nuclear developers to keep their nuclear weapons and casting later nuclear developers' efforts as illegitimate, the treaty created an unfair double standard.

The superpowers, among others, argued that the NPT was necessary to limit the spread of nuclear weapons that threatened international peace. The Soviets pressured North Korea to sign the NPT, and accelerated this pressure in the early 1980s when North Korea was constructing a nuclear complex at Yongbyon. In 1985, North Korea finally relented and signed the treaty in exchange for Soviet aid, including a promise to supply another type of nuclear reactor that did not pose the same nuclear weapons concerns. North Korea's signing the NPT, along with its pledges to submit to International Atomic Energy Agency (IAEA) safeguards, led the US intelligence community to conclude in 1987 that North Korea's "development of a nuclear weapon is constrained."[8] In 1989, the CIA still described North Korea's nuclear development as primarily intended for civilian purposes with possible future applications for military uses.[9] The assessment would change dramatically in the 1990s as the first North Korean nuclear crisis ensued.

What was the first North Korean nuclear crisis?

The first North Korean nuclear crisis comprised a set of events between 1992 and 1994, when North Korea sought to break out of the constraints on its nuclear development, making unambiguous moves toward nuclear weapons. North Korea could previously claim that its nuclear development was intended for peaceful purposes, and the international community could have some measure of relief that North Korean moves to shift to a weapons program would be detectable. The first nuclear crisis was the detection of those very moves.

In September 1991, President George H. W. Bush announced that the United States would remove its tactical nuclear weapons from South Korea.[10] North Korea had previously refused unilateral denuclearization, but the United States' tactical nuclear weapons withdrawal allowed Seoul and Pyongyang to agree to the denuclearization of the entire Korean Peninsula. A landmark inter-Korean agreement in December 1991, colloquially referred to as the Basic Agreement, pledged to pursue inter-Korean rapprochement and the "elimination of weapons of mass destruction" from Korea. The two Koreas expanded upon this pledge the following month with a stand-alone denuclearization pledge. Neither side would "test, manufacture, produce, receive, possess, store, deploy, or use nuclear weapons."[11]

Ten days after North Korea signed the inter-Korean denuclearization pledge, it submitted its long-overdue nuclear safeguards agreement to the UN's nuclear watchdog, the IAEA. The North submitted its nuclear declaration three months after that, in May 1992. The IAEA detected "inconsistencies" in the "completeness and correctness" of North Korea's claims and demanded special inspections in February 1993. North Korea refused, calling the inspections an unprecedented violation of state sovereignty. North Korea threatened to withdraw from the NPT in March 1993, effectively threatening that it would not forgo nuclear weapons development. The IAEA declared North Korea to be in noncompliance of its nuclear safeguards agreement and referred the matter to the UN Security Council, which had authority to impose sanctions and other punishments. In May 1993, the UN Security Council called on North Korea to comply with its nuclear safeguards agreement.

Meanwhile, the United States and North Korea negotiated the matter. In June 1993, the two countries reached an agreement that the United States would not attack North Korea or interfere in its internal affairs, and North Korea would reaffirm its denuclearization commitments and rejoin the NPT. IAEA inspectors returned to North Korea to verify that the country was upholding its commitments. North Korean authorities refused IAEA inspectors access to critical facilities in 1994, and North Korea removed spent fuel rods from its

5MW reactor at Yongbyon without the inspectors present. This was a critical move, because reprocessing the spent fuel rods would give North Korea the materials it needed to build a nuclear weapon, and all sides knew it. The averted crisis began anew.

The crisis had reached an acute stage, and there was credible threat of war on the peninsula. Former US president Jimmy Carter traveled to Pyongyang to meet with the ailing North Korean leader Kim Il Sung in June 1994. The United States and North Korea agreed to negotiate the matter. Kim Il Sung died the following month, but his eldest son and successor, Kim Jong Il, continued the diplomatic engagement. American and North Korean negotiators continued to meet until October 1994, when they signed the 1994 Agreed Framework outlining North Korea's nuclear freeze.

What was the US-DPRK Agreed Framework?

The US-DPRK Agreed Framework was a bilateral agreement signed in 1994 to freeze North Korea's nuclear weapons program. It delayed and degraded North Korea's nuclear infrastructure but did not end North Korea's nuclear ambitions or its pursuit of the bomb. In exchange for the nuclear freeze, North Korea received significant energy and economic assistance, as well as security guarantees and promises to establish diplomatic relations.

During the negotiation and implementation of the Agreed Framework, North Korea noted (correctly) that it faced a severe energy shortage. It argued that it needed nuclear energy to rectify this matter, which was a highly suspect claim. North Korea's preferred nuclear-power option could not resolve its energy shortage for a variety of technical reasons, including the aging North Korean electrical grid's inability to transmit power from the proposed nuclear plants and much more cost-effective and efficient alternative sources of energy. Nevertheless, North Korean negotiators maintained that this was their sovereign decision. They wanted nuclear power for energy, medical, and general scientific advancement purposes that they claimed could provide their country long-term economic benefits. Consequently, energy aid was a top North Korean demand.

The two countries agreed to "replace" North Korea's plutonium reactors at Yongbyon, which could allow North Korea to produce nuclear weapons, with two more-modern light-water reactors (LWRs), which were not suitable to nuclear weapons development. In the time it took to build the LWRs, the United States would arrange through a multilateral consortium to provide heavy fuel oil to North Korea to make up for the purported energy loss from Yongbyon. In practice, South Korea and Japan would pay much of the bill for the energy consortium after the Republican-controlled Congress balked at the Clinton administration's deal.

Beyond providing energy aid, the United States also agreed to ease economic sanctions, move toward establishing diplomatic relations with North Korea, and provide formal assurances that it would not use nuclear weapons against North Korea. North Korea agreed to allow IAEA inspectors to monitor its nuclear freeze, rejoin the NPT, "consistently take steps" toward denuclearization, and return to full compliance with the IAEA safeguards agreement.

The Agreed Framework had a mixed record of accomplishment. It resulted in a verified eight-year freeze of North Korea's plutonium program, and only North Korea's most developed but smallest nuclear reactor survived the deal. North Korea had two larger plutonium reactors under construction in 1994 that did not survive years of shutdown. However, North Korea also initiated a second route to the bomb via uranium enrichment. The United States also had difficulty upholding its side of the bargain as the construction of the LWRs and progress toward diplomatic recognition slowed, and both sides pointed fingers at the other for undermining the agreement first.

Why did the United States give North Korea aid?

The United States provided aid to North Korea as part of nuclear agreements and in response to North Korean humanitarian emergencies. Washington provided energy and economic aid in the late 1990s in accordance with the 1994 Agreed Framework freezing North Korea's nuclear weapons program. The United States also provided humanitarian assistance in the form of food and medicine in the same time period, which corresponded with North Korea's famine. The United States also provided North Korea with energy and economic assistance as part of the 2005 Six Party Talks agreement. It promised "nutritional assistance" simultaneously with North Korean nuclear and missile pledges in a 2012 agreement, although the agreement fell apart before the United States delivered any aid. Washington has maintained that it bases humanitarian aid decisions on demonstrated humanitarian need and aid availability exclusively as mandated by American law and humanitarian principles, but some observers note that aid rises and falls with political agreements on the nuclear and missile programs.

More specifically, the Congressional Research Service tabulated that the United States provided North Korea 1.3 billion dollars' worth of aid from 1995 to 2008. This time frame corresponds with the Agreed Framework and Six Party Talks. This sum does not include billions of dollars of energy aid that the United States encouraged South Korea and Japan to fund to implement the Agreed Framework in the late 1990s. The United States directly provided North Korea with approximately 600 million dollars' worth of energy aid between 1995 and 2003 as part of the Agreed Framework and between 2007 and 2009 as part of the Six Party Talks. The United States provided over $700 million in food and medicine to North Korea, primarily during and following the country's late 1990s famine.[12]

Providing North Korea aid has been controversial in the United States and abroad. Proponents point to the benefits it has elicited on nuclear agreements, if only partial and temporary, and the moral obligation to help the North Korean people when their government has failed to do so. However, some critics charge that the aid kept the country afloat at its deepest point of crisis and precluded the otherwise inevitable collapse of a morally bankrupt government. Others criticize the expense, noting that the aid money could have been more appropriately spent on other domestic or foreign priorities. A variation on this theme maintains that Washington, Seoul, and Tokyo could have used the aid to provide food and medicine to other countries with greater humanitarian needs, negating the moral argument of being for or against feeding the hungry. Still others show that North Korea reduced its commercial food imports as foreign food aid increased, demonstrating a moral hazard in that the North Korean government avoids enacting politically difficult economic reforms needed to supply the basic needs of its people knowing that the international community will step in to help in a pinch.

North Korea unquestionably has an energy shortage and a chronic food problem. Energy aid has been used to elicit North Korean promises about its nuclear program, and there is a strong argument to be made that humanitarian assistance has likely been politicized for this purpose too. However, the question of providing aid to North Korea is more complex than a simple calculation of feeding the hungry, providing medicine to the sick, or heat to the cold. It involves difficult pragmatic trade-offs and moral determinations about which reasonable people will disagree.

When did North Korea start testing missiles to hit the United States?

North Korea's ballistic missile program goes back decades, but it began flight-testing long-range missiles in 1998. Ballistic missile development involves building the airframes, testing the engines, checking for accuracy, and an array of scientific and technical tasks. But the most observable action is when a country decides to launch a prototype to see if a missile they think works actually does. North Korea developed its Taepo Dong-1 rocket by stacking its previous, shorter-range missiles on top of each other. When the first stage of the rocket stopped thrusting, the second stage was supposed to separate from the first and push the rocket farther to extend its range. North Korean rocket scientists could not know for sure whether they had accomplished their goal until they tried launching it.

In 1998, North Korea launched its Taepo Dong-1 long-range rocket from its territory eastward over Japan. The missile's airframe splashed down in the Pacific Ocean. The flight test rattled Japan, in particular, which saw a neighboring country deeply hostile to it testing increasingly sophisticated missiles. However, North Korea could already strike Japan with its operational Nodong missile at the time, which posed a greater threat to the country than the developmental prototype Taepo Dong-1. Nevertheless, the launch jump-started Japanese cooperation with the United States on missile defense. It also ushered in a new round of high-level US–North Korea diplomacy focused on missiles.

The United States and North Korea negotiated to limit North Korea's missile program, culminating in the US secretary of state Madeleine Albright's visiting Pyongyang in October 2000 in preparation for a possible presidential visit that never transpired. Nevertheless, North Korea agreed in 1999 to suspend long-range missile launches while the US–North Korea talks progressed in exchange for some economic sanctions relief. After the talks broke down as the Clinton administration transitioned into the Bush administration in 2001, North Korea continued to abide by its long-range missile launch moratorium, until 2006.

On the Fourth of July in 2006, North Korea lit some fireworks. It launched a series of missiles, including a Taepo Dong-2 developmental rocket that failed shortly after launch. It launched the rocket again three years later, in April 2009, with more success, but failed in the third effort in April 2012. North Korea seemed to work out the kinks, and they successfully launched the rocket and put a satellite into space in December 2012 and February 2016. The Taepo Dong was a static rocket launched from a known launch pad and was not a weapon that could be used in a crisis. Air strikes could take it out. But it was a critical part of North Korea's research and development effort to build and field a road-mobile variant missile that could strike the continental United States.

Understanding North Korea's earlier research and development efforts requires some explanation of what constitutes a "rocket." For example, NASA (and its international partners) launch astronauts into outer space on rockets for peaceful, civilian purposes. The US Department of Defense's long-range ballistic missiles are also rockets. Both civilian "space launch vehicles" and military "missiles" use similar technology to propel a "rocket" upward and breach the atmosphere.

North Korea claimed its rocket launches were civilian "space launches" intended to put satellites into orbit. Indeed, the North Koreans successfully put two satellites into orbit on their later launches. However, the UN Security Council has recognized that any North Korean launches that test and develop ballistic-missile-related technology are a threat. Its earlier claims notwithstanding, North Korea does not aim to become a space-faring country looking at other planets and conducting scientific research; rather they are building a missile force as part of their national defense. They have used the knowledge from these earlier rocket launches in subsequent flight tests that North Korea has explicitly recognized as intercontinental ballistic missiles (ICBMs) to put the United States in range of North Korea's nuclear weapons.

A key difference between a space-launch vehicle and a missile is the ability to place a warhead on top and have the missile re-enter Earth's atmosphere and carry the warhead toward a target. This is the last main challenge North Korea needs to meet to achieve a true ICBM capability. It can get a warhead up into the sky, but to have a functioning missile, it needs to be able to demonstrate that it can get a nuclear bomb back down through the stresses of atmospheric re-entry and have it hit a specific target. North Korea claimed it had completed its ICBM development after three launches in 2017. This statement was likely premature. But US officials have noted publicly that North Korea needs just a few more months of active development work, when that flight testing work resumes, to complete its ICBM. At the time of final review of this book in January 2019, North Korea's flight testing has not yet resumed.

Has North Korea sold long-range missiles to other countries?

North Korea has sold short- and medium-range ballistic missiles to a variety of countries, primarily in the Middle East, for decades. However, there is no solid evidence at the time of writing that North Korea has sold its most advanced and long-range missiles abroad. This may be, in part, because of a lack of customers or North Korea's desire to keep its most advanced technology out of the hands of others that could reveal technical secrets of the systems or seek to replicate the more advanced missiles on their own.

North Korea sold short-range ballistic missiles called SCUDs to virtually anyone who would buy them in the 1980s. Most of its customers were in the Middle East. North Korea sold military technology to Iraq in the 1970s; after Iraq invaded neighboring Iran in 1980, sparking an eight-year war that used up many ballistic missiles on both sides, North Korea sold SCUDs to Iran as the war dragged on. North Korea also sold ballistic missiles or their components to Egypt, Libya, Yemen, Pakistan, and others. They also benefited from ballistic missile development cooperation with some of its customers as well as Russia and China.

The 1991 Gulf War, when the United States decisively forced Iraq to retreat from its invasion of neighboring Kuwait, demonstrated to many countries in the region that ballistic missiles were increasingly obsolete. Iraq's ballistic missiles did not prevent its defeat. As the Middle Eastern states shifted to more advanced weapons, North Korea lost customers. However, some customers remained, most notably Iran, which had a desire for medium-range ballistic missiles that could reach farther.

North Korea helped Iran to develop medium-range ballistic missiles that can reach Israel and parts of southeast Europe. The two business partners are deeply skeptical of each other, and Iran has sought to develop its missiles indigenously wherever it can. This has included Iran's reverse engineering North Korea's technology while North Korea has sought to keep its most lucrative missile buyer coming back for more. Given the two countries' willingness to buy and sell ballistic missiles of increasing range over the years, it is reasonable to speculate that North Korea's selling Iran long-range missiles that can reach all of Europe and the United States may be the next step in their relationship. However, there is no public evidence that they have done so yet.

Why did the US-DPRK Agreed Framework collapse?

The 1994 US-DPRK Agreed Framework was beset with implementation challenges on both sides until its final demise in late 2002 and early 2003. Each side blamed the other for the collapse. The United States said that North Korea cheated by initiating a second, secret route to the bomb. North Korea complained that the United States slow-rolled and did not provide all the energy and political concessions it had agreed to supply. Both sets of facts are correct, and the mutual finger-pointing meant the agreement's days were numbered.

North Korea promised in 1994 to take specific steps to freeze its then only route to the bomb. It shut down its plutonium reactor at Yongbyon, which international inspectors verified. However, it secretly began a uranium enrichment program during the Agreed Framework implementation years that violated North Korea's general commitment to denuclearization. Reports from North Korean defectors claim that

Pyongyang began this effort in 1996; an unclassified CIA report to Congress put the start date closer to 2000.[13] Regardless, North Korea cheated.

The United States promised in 1994 to provide North Korea with two LWRs and to work to establish diplomatic relations with North Korea, among other things. The United States created an international consortium of states to finance the project, of which South Korea and Japan paid the most. However, the LWR construction was delayed leading to North Korean consternation. In addition, the United States promised to establish a liaison office in Pyongyang and to work toward ambassadorial-level relations. Though there were internal preparations to do so, Washington never opened this diplomatic facility in Pyongyang.

The change of presidential administration from Bill Clinton to George W. Bush in 2001 also changed the level of American support for the agreement. The Bush administration was deeply divided on North Korea policy, especially in its first term (2001–2005).[14] Shortly after President Bush's inauguration in 2001, US secretary of state Colin Powell had to walk back some public comments in which he had said the United States intended to pick up where the Clinton administration had left off on North Korea policy. The Bush administration conducted a policy review that validated Powell's original statements, but the sentiment shifted to favor the hawks within the administration after terrorists struck the United States on September 11, 2001.

The Bush administration's top diplomat on Asia traveled to Pyongyang in October 2002, having little room to negotiate, and he returned noting that the North Koreans admitted to pursuing a second route to the bomb. The North Koreans denied saying this, and the nature of the conversation became a subject of controversy. Regardless of the specific conversation, public evidence now corroborates what US officials claimed at the time: North Korea had a second path to the bomb in violation of its denuclearization commitments.

Following this October 2002 meeting, the international consortium providing fuel oil to North Korea as part of the US commitment under the deal stopped its shipments at the request of the United States. North Korea said the United States had abrogated the Agreed Framework. In December 2002, North Korea announced that it would restart the nuclear facilities frozen under the agreement and expelled international nuclear inspectors. The following month, they announced their intent to withdraw from the Nuclear Nonproliferation Treaty—the country's most significant legal commitment to forgo nuclear weapons. The Agreed Framework was dead.

What was the second North Korean nuclear crisis?

The collapse of the Agreed Framework in late 2002 and early 2003 initiated the second North Korean nuclear crisis. The first crisis had taken place in the early 1990s as North Korea moved to reprocess spent fuel rods in its nuclear reactor at Yongbyon that could be used in nuclear weapons. The Agreed Framework froze that reactor, but the deal's dismantling and North Korea's restarting the reactor renewed the crisis. This time, North Korea had not only its established plutonium reactor running again but also a nascent uranium enrichment path to the bomb under way as well.

The United States under President George W. Bush did not like the Agreed Framework. Some of the president's hard-line advisers stated their preference for regime change, but the administration never adopted such a policy. The president's national security adviser and, later, secretary of state, Condoleezza Rice, recognized in her memoirs that the nation's top military advisers wanted no part of military action on the Korean Peninsula, warning of the high costs of another war in Korea.[15] President Bush authorized a new round of diplomacy with North Korea, backed by a series of efforts to enhance the economic pressure on Pyongyang, in search of a better agreement. Instead of a temporary freeze of the North's nuclear facilities, Bush wanted something more lasting and comprehensive. He called it "complete, verifiable, irreversible denuclearization" (CVID).

What were the Six Party Talks?

The Six Party Talks were a multilateral forum that brought together the United States, North Korea, South Korea, China, Japan, and Russia to work toward the denuclearization of the Korean Peninsula. China chaired the forum, so the main meetings, when the lead negotiators of each of the countries met, were in Beijing. The six parties began meeting in 2003 and produced the Joint Statement of the Six Party Talks in 2005 and two implementation agreements in 2007. The talks collapsed in 2008.

The first major achievement of the Six Party Talks was the 2005 Joint Statement. It laid out the broad principles of North Korea's denuclearization and the reciprocal steps that North Korea required from the others to secure its denuclearization actions. The other five parties "stated their willingness to provide energy assistance" to North Korea and "discuss, at an appropriate time, the subject of the provision of light water reactor [sic]" to North Korea. The United States and North Korea pledged peaceful coexistence and agreed to "take steps to normalize" their diplomatic relations. Japan and North Korea made a similar pledge on diplomatic relations. "The directly related parties will negotiate a permanent peace regime on the Korean Peninsula at an appropriate separate forum."[16]

Negotiators haggled over each phrase, and the ambiguity in many of the commitments was purposeful. A pledge to discuss a peace regime, for example, is very different than agreeing to conclude one. Likewise, noting that the "directly related parties" would participate—when peace treaty negotiations had broken down since 1953 on the question of which parties were "directly related"—also showed that the Joint Statement left many issues to be resolved. The promise to "discuss, at an appropriate time," the provision to North Korea of "light water reactor" opened the door to a predictable dispute over when the five parties, and specifically, the United States, would actually provide North Korea this reactor or reactors. The North Koreans argued that the appropriate time was immediately; the United States preferred a distant point in the future. All sides knew that the devil was in the details, and the 2005 agreement left many of those details for future negotiations. Nevertheless, it was a start. The Joint Statement provided a basis—a highly imperfect basis—on which the six countries could push forward on specifics. The 2005 agreement was not an operational agreement. It was a set of principles. A year and a half later, in February 2007, the six parties produced their first operational agreement, giving it the technocratic title, "Initial Actions for the Implementation of the Joint Statement."

In February 2007, North Korea agreed to seal its Yongbyon reactor and allow international inspectors to verify the reactor's shutdown. At this time, the United States also specified its sanctions relief and details about the heavy fuel oil that North Korea would receive in exchange for its nuclear moves. The six countries agreed to a series of working group meetings to discuss the core areas of each sides' demands: denuclearization, normalization of US-DPRK relations, normalization of Japan-DPRK relations, economic and energy assistance, and a peace regime. The United States and its allies were most interested in the denuclearization subject, while the North Koreans saw the other four working groups as advancing its goals. The six parties agreed to meet again once each side had carried outs its "initial actions."[17]

The six-party process was making concrete progress toward denuclearization as North Korea sealed its Yongbyon reactor, and international inspectors verified the shutdown. North Korea likewise found the forward movement on its demands sufficiently acceptable to continue. The six parties met eight months after the February 2017 agreement, "confirmed the implementation of the initial actions" had indeed been carried out, and laid the roadmap for the next step. In October 2017, they agreed to the not-so-creatively titled "Second-Phase Actions for the Implementation of the September 2005 Joint Statement."[18]

In October 2017, in the second-phase agreement, North Korea agreed to complete the disablement of "all existing nuclear facilities subject to abandonment" and to allow a US expert group to visit Yongbyon to prepare for disablement. "Disablement" meant going beyond simply turning out the lights at the Yongbyon reactor. Disablement involved taking apart some of the reactor's plumbing. The North Koreans could reverse disablement in six months or so, but it was a step beyond a simple shutdown and short of full denuclearization.

The devil was still in the details, and even the more specific agreements left large areas of ambiguity or papering over of differences. For example, North Korea's agreement to disable "all existing nuclear facilities subject to abandonment" reads unnaturally and like something that multiple people wrote, because it was. The United States opted to focus on North Korea's more developed plutonium program for disablement and to not get bogged down at this stage in North Korea's separate uranium enrichment program. The disablement procedures focused on Yongbyon specified the facilities subject to abandonment without either side having to reach agreement on the existence or legitimacy of North Korea's uranium program.

However, North Korea also promised a "complete and correct declaration of all its nuclear programs in accordance with the February 13 agreement." Contemporary news reports quoted anonymous American officials who claimed that North Korea had said in a secret agreement that it would come clean about its uranium enrichment and the proliferation of nuclear technology to Syria, but Pyongyang never publicly acknowledged such a separate understanding.[19]

In May 2008, Pyongyang provided an 18,000-page declaration of its nuclear programs, and the next month dramatically destroyed its cooling tower in front of the assembled international press. However, Washington said that it would need to verify the North Korean nuclear declaration, which all sides had agreed would have to be "complete" and "correct." The United States noted that the declaration was neither complete nor correct; North Korea said it was. The United States demanded a scientific sampling of the soil around the nuclear facilities and nuclear waste to prove it. North Korea refused, noting this demand was not written into the second-phase agreement. North Korea's foreign ministry suggested that it might be willing to allow sampling as part of a third-phase agreement, presumably in tandem with concrete advancement of its own demands, but the two sides deadlocked. In December 2008, the six parties met for the last time as they could not reach agreement on the sequencing for or generally acceptability of scientific sampling.[20] The Six Party Talks remained talks in name only after that as the active diplomatic process stopped.

Has North Korea proliferated nuclear technology to other countries?

Yes. North Korea has proliferated nuclear technology to Syria directly and to Libya indirectly. Some argue that North Korea could provide nuclear technology to Iran as well, but there is no evidence of a nuclear proliferation relationship to date.[21] However, there should be little doubt about North Korea's willingness to sell the building blocks of a nuclear weapons program to other countries, since they have already done so.

Syria. In September 2007, Israeli air strikes destroyed a nuclear reactor that was nearing completion in a remote part of Syria. The Syrian reactor lacked critical infrastructure necessary for a nuclear reactor that could produce electricity or scientific research, and the Syrians made a series of efforts to try to conceal its location. For over a decade, North Korea had cooperated with Syria on nuclear matters. Prior to the beginning of construction of the Syria reactor in 2001, a senior delegation from North Korea's Yongbyon nuclear complex visited Syria; North Korean procurement networks started buying equipment for the Syrian reactor in 2002; and a series of Syrian and North Korean delegations visited each other in the coming years. After the Israeli air strikes, another senior North Korean delegation visited Syria and met Syrian nuclear officials. Rather than continually object to Israel's attack on its territory, Syria instead attempted to cover up the evidence of its nuclear weapons program while claiming it never had one.

The Syrian reactor, viewed from satellites before and after its destruction, showed that it was modeled on North Korea's Yongbyon reactor. No other country had built this type of reactor in thirty-five years, and specific components of the North Korean and Syrian reactors were the same.

The CIA declassified the details of its assessment in April 2008 to brief Congress. The agency created a short video of the unclassified assessment, which was posted on YouTube.[22] Once it was declassified, CIA Director Mike Hayden issued a statement to all CIA employees on the intelligence success and congratulated all who had been involved in the assessment.[23] Years later, he highlighted the discovery of North Korea's support of Syria's reactor for a Syrian nuclear weapons program as an incontrovertible case where US intelligence got it right.[24] As far as intelligence assessments go, the evidence that North Korea was supporting a Syrian nuclear weapons program is as clear as it gets.

Libya. North Korea may have assisted—wittingly or not—Libya's nuclear weapons program before Tripoli gave up its nuclear program in 2003. Libyan dictator Muammar Gaddafi had pursued nuclear technology for decades, courting a variety of potential foreign suppliers. Although the details are not as clear as they were for North Korea's nuclear cooperation with Syria, revelations of North Korea's indirect nuclear cooperation with Libya had surfaced years before the Syria connection, providing the first evidence that Pyongyang might be willing to share nuclear secrets and technology with other states. Libya appeared to get some of the necessary fuel for its uranium enrichment program through the network of Abdul Qadeer (A. Q.) Khan. A. Q. Khan was the father of Pakistan's nuclear bomb and later went into a dangerous and illegal business of selling nuclear secrets and technology to foreign states. His customers included North Korea and Libya, among others. Khan's nuclear business was a network, and North Korea seemingly provided Khan uranium hexafluoride (UF6). UF6 is a necessary ingredient for uranium enrichment to produce nuclear bombs.

It is not clear whether the North Koreans knew where this uranium was headed. However, US officials, speaking after Gaddafi had given up his nuclear weapons program and subjected his nuclear technology to American technical exploitation, said that North Korea's UF6 did end up in Libya's program.[25] The White House press secretary later noted, "Whether the intended recipient was the Khan network or Libya is irrelevant to our proliferation concerns regarding North Korea. The fact that nuclear material found its way out of North Korea to any destination is a source of serious concern."[26]

Why did the Six Party Talks stalemate?

China convened the Six Party Talks in Beijing from 2003 to 2008. In late 2008, the United States demanded a scientific sampling of soil and nuclear waste at North Korea's nuclear facilities to verify that its nuclear declaration was "complete and correct," as promised. North Korea refused, noting that sampling was not part of the two implementation agreements penned to date. The North Koreans suggested that scientific sampling should wait for the third implementation agreement that would presumably require further concessions from the American side in return. The Americans saw verification of North Korea's claims as part and parcel of the agreement. The two sides reached an impasse, and the Six Party Talks never convened again.

For the next few years, all sides continued to refer to the Six Party Talks. The various parties met at different times to set the conditions for diplomacy, and all sides maintained their Six Party Talks negotiators. The United States and North Korea even met bilaterally ahead of a short-lived 2012 agreement, but the six countries never revived the defunct six party process.

When and why did North Korea conduct nuclear tests?

North Korea conducted six nuclear tests between 2006 and 2017, which helped advance its effort to build reliable nuclear weapons. Building nuclear weapons is a complex endeavor, and weapons scientists and political leaders alike want to make sure the devices operate as intended. Consequently, states pursuing nuclear weapons have invariably sought to detonate them to make sure they work. Tests can diagnose problem areas or allow a country to build and refine increasingly sophisticated types of nuclear weapons.

North Korea has conducted all six of its nuclear tests to date at the Punggye-ri nuclear test site. The test site is simply a set of tunnels under a mountain in the northeast of North Korea, toward its border with China. All North Korea's nuclear tests have been underground, which is a common means of limiting the environmental and health consequences of nuclear testing while also concealing certain technical details of the tests from watchful foreign adversaries. Nuclear explosions are so powerful that they create tremors in the earth called "artificial earthquakes." International monitors can and do pick up indications of North Korea's nuclear tests, and the North Koreans have publicly confirmed each test.

North Korea's first nuclear test in 2006 was the most politically significant. It demonstrated a willful decision in Pyongyang to cross a threshold and move from a theoretical nuclear capability to a demonstrated one. However, North Korea's first nuclear test created more of a whimper than a bang. It produced a "low yield," meaning that it was not as large an explosion as nuclear experts would expect from a genuine nuclear bomb. North Korea conducted its second nuclear test in 2009 and seemed to have worked out the kinks. On this try, they demonstrated an ability to successfully detonate a nuclear device. North Korea still could not mount that weapon on a long-range missile and hurl it toward an intercontinental target like the United States, but it had crossed the nuclear weapons threshold.

With its third nuclear test in 2013, North Korea demonstrated a still larger yield. In January 2016, North Korea claimed that its fourth test demonstrated a thermonuclear capability, which offers substantially greater destructive power than an atomic blast. In September 2016, North Korea's fifth test accelerated the pacing of the tests. There had been about three years between the previous nuclear tests, but this one followed the previous test by only eight months. In September 2017, North Korea conducted its sixth and final nuclear test before North Korean leader Kim Jong Un declared his nuclear weapons effort complete. In May 2018, Kim demolished his only known nuclear testing site.

What is North Korea's byungjin policy?

In 2013, North Korean leader Kim Jong Un delivered a major address in which he reintroduced the Korean concept of *byungjin*, or the simultaneous development of North Korea's economy and nuclear weapons. Kim Jong Un's grandfather, Kim Il Sung, had first established the *byungjin* policy in the 1960s, but his version spoke about the simultaneous development of North Korea's economy and conventional military. Nonetheless, the basic premise—that Pyongyang would not have to forgo economic development to meet its defense goals—was the same. Economists speak about the trade-offs in national budgets between investing in "guns" (defense) versus "butter" (domestic social priorities), but Kim Jong Un rejected this framework and asserted that the country could have both.

Kim Jong Un's *byungjin* policy rejected the premise that had undergirded earlier denuclearization efforts. The United States and its partners offered North Korea an alternative future. If Pyongyang rejected nuclear development and relied on its conventional forces for its defense, then North Korea could reap the economic rewards of sanctions relief and reintegration in the global economy. Kim Jong Un effectively argued that the North Koreans could stand on their own resources to rebuild their economy, reject the "belt-tightening" austerity that had been common in previous years, and have their cake and eat it too. He even argued that nuclear development would advance the country's science and technology platform to bring broader economic benefits.

Byungjin was short lived. Kim learned that he could develop the North Korean economy without international economic pressure relief, but it would have certain limits. North Korea could enjoy modest economic growth by improving domestic production and efficiency measures, but it would not lift the country out of its impoverished state. Although his precise motives continue to be debated, Kim Jong Un decided at the beginning of 2018 to reach out to South Korea and the United States. In exchange for denuclearization, Kim Jong Un agreed in principle with US President Donald Trump that North Korea would enjoy the end of US–South Korea military exercises, security guarantees, and economic sanctions relief. At least in this US–North Korea summit declaration, Kim Jong Un had returned to the old rubric that recognized trade-offs between nuclear and economic development.

Analysts vehemently disagree on whether Kim is genuinely willing to forgo his nuclear program to advance his economy (in tandem with receiving tangible security guarantees) or whether the latest round of diplomacy is just Kim's tactical rouse to weaken international economic and military pressure, while he resists any meaningful reduction of his nuclear capabilities. The difference is central to policy choices being made in Washington and elsewhere, but the effect on North Korea's stated nuclear doctrine is the same: Kim Jong Un's open rejection of the fundamental trade-off between his country's economic and nuclear development that characterized the *byungjin* policy has been sidelined.

Can North Korea strike the United States with nuclear weapons?

North Korea has for decades pursued a nuclear weapons project and long-range ballistic missile development. Both efforts have been explicitly targeted at the United States, which North Korea considers its most pressing security threat. In 2018, senior American officials repeatedly noted that North Korea is a "handful of months" away from developing a capability of striking the continental United States with nuclear weapons.[27] It does not appear that North Korea can reach the continental United States currently, but it is perilously close. North Korea does have America's treaty allies South Korea and Japan within missile range, including the tens of thousands American troops stationed in the two countries. North Korea can also reach the American territory of Guam, which houses a significant American military presence as well, and it has claimed that its missiles can reach Alaska and Hawaii.

North Korea has made considerable strides in its nuclear development and rocket technology efforts. Both are complex areas of science that have evaded the capabilities of most countries in the world. North Korea is not a simple and backward military dictatorship, but a ruthless regime with significant technological capabilities. It has shown unmistakably through nuclear tests that it can detonate nuclear devices. It has also shown through missile flight tests, which the United States and its allies have tracked, that it can fly rockets with increasingly long ranges. Intercontinental ballistic missiles breach the atmosphere and re-enter it to descend toward their targets. North Korea has shown its ability to send the rockets up, but it still needs to demonstrate that it can reliably bring them back down toward a specific target.

Part of the challenge of bringing a missile back down toward a target has to do with re-entry stress. The missile experiences tremendous pressure as it re-enters Earth's atmosphere, and ensuring that a nuclear device mounted on the tip will function as intended during this time is a difficult challenge. Also, a missile must be accurate to be effective. The nuclear-tipped missile must not be able to simply hit somewhere in the ocean but to strike a particular target. North Korea has attempted to compensate for its missile accuracy issues by building higher-yield nuclear weapons that can still destroy targets even if they miss the bullseye. At the same time, they need to keep the weapon light enough to avoid reducing the missile's range.

North Korea has claimed that it has already hurdled these obstacles. Kim Jong Un declared his integrated nuclear deterrent complete in November 2017 and again in his major New Year's Day address on January 1, 2018. However, he has not demonstrated fully these capabilities, leaving American officials to note publicly that Pyongyang is close but not quite there yet. North Korea's pledge in 2018 to forgo additional nuclear tests and ballistic missile flight tests is important to limit the program's advancement beyond the last remaining obstacles. It remains to be seen if the US–North Korea diplomacy kicked off at the first ever US–North Korea summit on June 12, 2018 in Singapore will block and roll back North Korea's nuclear threat to the continental United States.

Can North Korea strike South Korea and Japan with nuclear weapons?

South Korea and Japan are within North Korea's missile range. South Korea's capital of Seoul is within North Korean artillery range too. When North Korea started acquiring and developing short-range ballistic missiles in the 1970s and mass producing them in the 1980s, North Korea could strike virtually anywhere in South Korea. Though North Korea lacked nuclear weapons at these earlier times, the regime could put chemical weapons on the warheads to deliver weapons of mass destruction (WMD) reliably to anywhere in South Korea. South Korea has lived with the North Korean WMD threat to its security longer than any other country.

In the 1980s, North Korea moved to expand the range of its ballistic missiles. It started developing the Nodong intermediate-range ballistic missile, which it deployed in 1995. The Nodong put Japan in range of North Korea's WMD-tipped missiles. However, North Korea's 1998 launch of the Taepo-Dong 1 prototype rocket, which overflew Japan, stimulated the greatest Japanese response to North Korea's missile threat. In reality, North Korea at the time of the Taepo Dong 1 launch could already strike Japan with operational and deployed missiles, and the Taepo Dong 1 was still just a research and development effort. Assuming that North Korea has made its nuclear weapons small and light enough to fit atop a missile, which appears reasonable at the ranges required to strike South Korea or Japan, North Korea can hit both nations with nuclear-tipped missiles today.

What does North Korea seek from nuclear weapons?

North Korea articulates its nuclear weapons primarily as a deterrent against US invasion. Pyongyang has repeatedly noted that the United States invaded Iraq and supported the rebellion in Libya, which led to the downfall of both regimes because the two countries could not threaten massive retaliation against the American homeland. If North Korea can strike the United States with nuclear weapons, then it does not need to worry about an American regime-change effort. North Korea is less concerned about South Korea, which North Korea believes it can keep in check with a direct artillery threat to

South Korea's capital and roughly equivalent aggregate conventional military power. North Korea has known that it is no match for the American military's conventional forces, especially since seeing their decisive victory over Saddam Hussein's seemingly formidable military in the 1991 Gulf War using superior American technology, and it has come to rely on nuclear weapons to deter Washington.

Beyond deterrence, North Korean leader Kim Jong Un has made comments suggesting that he sees nuclear weapons as a tool of national defense beyond deterrence. New nuclear powers, including the United States in the 1950s, have sought ways to use these hard-won weapons for purposes other than simply providing the ultimate insurance policy against invasion. Kim Jong Un called nuclear weapons instruments of national power that should allow Pyongyang to translate other objectives in foreign affairs into a reality. In other words, Kim suggested that he intended to use his nuclear arsenal to coerce other states, such as South Korea, to bend to his will. It is not clear how he intended to do so, and other states have had a difficult time moving beyond deterrence to credibly coerce other foreign powers in this way, but it remains to be seen if North Korea will use its nuclear weapons to try to coerce more broadly.

North Korea has also used its nuclear program to capture the attention of the world's great powers and advance its interests in diplomatic negotiations with them. North Korea has repeatedly and credibly noted that it did not sacrifice for decades and face international isolation simply to trade away its nuclear weapons as a bargaining chip. However, North Korea has at times agreed to limit portions of its nuclear development and verifiably implemented some of those commitments to win security guarantees or sanctions relief. North Korea has called the United States its main security threat and demanded American involvement and concessions in all diplomatic efforts focused on North Korean denuclearization.

What does North Korea want from the United States?

North Korea says it wants an end to the United States' "hostile policy." The "hostile policy" is a vague concept that has changed to fit North Korean demands. In a nutshell, North Korea wants to feel secure and to see obstacles to unification on its terms removed, avoid economic pressure and enjoy economic aid, and operate its government as it sees fit without "foreign interference" in its "internal affairs."

North Korea deems the US military presence in South Korea threatening. It claims the American–South Korean military exercises, which practice defending South Korea in the case of North Korean invasion, are actually war rehearsals for an American regime-change effort like the one that overthrew Saddam Hussein in Iraq in 2003. It objects to any augmentation of US forces, including flying nuclear-capable bombers around the Korean Peninsula or bringing aircraft carrier strike groups into the area. More fundamentally, North Korea has called the permanent stationing of American troops on the Korean Peninsula illegitimate; for North Korea, South Korean authorities are simply the puppet government of the American imperialists, who are occupying Korean land and precluding unification. North Korea seeks to limit, and dreams of ending, the US military presence in South Korea.

North Korea also calls for a comprehensive end of US economic sanctions. The United States imposes an array of sanctions on North Korea because of its status as a communist and socialist state, human rights abuses, WMD development, ballistic missile proliferation, drug trafficking, counterfeiting of US currency and goods, support for terrorism, and many other reasons. The North Koreans understand that removing one set of sanctions just means that other overlapping sanctions already on the books take its place. Consequently, North Korea prefers to see a complete removal of US sanctions as part of ending its "hostile policy."

Beyond ending the restrictions on US and foreign firms from trading with North Korea by lifting sanctions, North Korea has also sought American and international aid. In nuclear negotiations with the United States, Pyongyang has sought energy assistance, including pledges to build for North Korea proliferation-resistant nuclear reactors and to deliver heavy fuel oil, food and medical aid, and more general pledges of trade and investment assistance.

Finally, North Korea wants to be free of American criticism, including on what it deems its "internal affairs." The United States and many other nations recognize North Korea's tremendous human rights abuses and criticize those practices. These nations seek to stand up for the universal values defined in the UN Charter and have authorized special investigations into North Korean human rights abuses. The UN's finding that North Korea's human rights abuses are so extreme as to constitute "crimes against humanity" led to a referral to the UN Security Council; without China's veto to protect North Korea, the move could have led to charging Kim Jong Un with crimes at the International Criminal Court. North Korea rejects any notion that it is abusing human rights, calls the charges politically motivated by its enemies without addressing specific allegations, and urges foreign nations effectively to "mind their own business" and not interfere in the country's internal affairs. North Korea sees the United States as leading the charge on the human rights front, demonstrating American "hostility."

5

KOREA–JAPAN RELATIONS

What is the lasting effect of Japan's colonization of Korea?

Japan's 1910–1945 colonization of Korea has had lasting social, political, and economic effects on both North and South Korea. Japan's historical treatment of Korea remains almost universally unpopular in both Koreas, and this history is a vivid and significant part of national life in South and North Korea today. Korean reaction to Japanese colonization is so strong that some historians have argued that this colonial experience marked the birth of modern Korean nationalism. Foreign occupiers suppressing their language, culture, and everyday lives led Koreans to develop a unique national identity and encouraged some to push for political independence for the Korean nation.

More concretely, public opinion polls in South Korea consistently show that Japan is one of the most disliked countries, despite linguistic and cultural similarities, aligned geopolitical interests and democratic forms of government, and deep trade and investment links. A live video stream of Dokdo Island, which South Korea administers and Japan claims as its territory and names Takeshima, can be found in South Korean government buildings, including in the waiting room of the presidential office. Visits by Japanese politicians to the controversial Yasukuni Shrine, a privately run Shinto religious site and museum that whitewashes Japanese twentieth-century history, can and has become a major diplomatic irritant. Both sides carefully choose their words in describing the Japanese military's forced conscription of foreign women, primarily Korean and Chinese, into sexual servitude during World War II. The two countries carefully review the school textbooks and commemorative public statues of the other—as well as textbooks and memorials in other countries, including the United States—to see how the next generation is learning about the past.

Koreans on both sides of the DMZ fundamentally agree on many of these denunciations of Japan. Criticisms of Japanese moves in the South Korean press are often mirrored in the North Korean official media. North Korean public opinion has a very different meaning than public opinion in democratic South Korea, and polling data is not available on these questions. But the North Korean government stance is deeply anti-Japanese. The Americans receive the brunt of North Korean government criticism, but Japan is second in line.

South Korean national security officials readily recognize that Japan plays an important part in the US-led defense structure in responding to possible North Korean aggression. However, South Korean politicians cannot accept including Japanese officials in a comprehensive set of military planning efforts out of fear of the possibility of Japanese forces returning to the Korean Peninsula. For years American officials have advocated increased trilateralism, meaning more US–Japan–South Korea joint military responses to their common North Korean threat. There have been some additional trilateral efforts, including trilateral diplomatic meetings, development projects, and humanitarian response efforts, but this historical memory has meant that both conservative and progressive South Korean administrations have repeatedly sought to limit the scope of this cooperation.

Koreans are also at the forefront, along with the Chinese, in objecting to loosening Japan's pacifist constitution. American officials and conservative Japanese generally want to see

Tokyo do more to provide for its own defense, recognizing that its post-1945 history shows a strong record of supporting peace, development, and democracy in Japan and around the world. Koreans and Chinese generally worry that a militarized Japan may return to its pre-1945 history of violent imperialism in the Asia-Pacific. North Korea and China correctly see Japan as a critical node in the US military alliance system in Asia and have a security interest in keeping Japan militarily weak. South Korea, as a critical part of the US military alliance system itself, is more conflicted between issues of national identity and security interests. Socially and politically, Japan's colonization of Korea is a living history with tremendous contemporary importance.

Economically, the Japanese colonial period left a mark on Korea. Japan mobilized and exploited Korean labor in an increasingly brutal way as World War II approached and progressed. Korea emerged from this experience in 1945 with a certain economic infrastructure that was important to its later economic development. In the North, in particular, the Japanese left behind hydroelectric dams, which continue to supply power to North Korea's woefully decrepit energy grid and industry, which North Korea's leader Kim Il Sung would resurrect after the Korean War to quickly grow its heavy industry.

South Korea did not inherit as much critical infrastructure from the colonial era. However, South Korea did borrow methods of organization and business enterprise from the Japanese, and it later accepted Japanese reparations by another name to help fuel its economic expansion. South Korean president Park Chung-hee jump-started South Korea's economic miracle. Having trained at a Japanese military academy and served in the Japanese military prior to Korea's liberation, Park faced political resistance when he tried to establish diplomatic relations with Japan in 1965. However, Park recognized that this diplomatic normalization, and the economic windfall it brought from Japan, was important to advance his vision of radically transforming and industrializing South Korea. Today, big business dominates the South Korean and Japanese economies in a way that is foreign to Americans. Entrepreneurship and small businesses are weak segments in both countries, which for decades have focused their development on a relatively small number of very large businesses. Both countries also have a legacy of tight big business–government relations that foreign corporations have repeatedly charged with being exclusionary. Even the internal organization of South Korean and Japanese big businesses and government bureaucracies is similar. It is impossible to say if South Korea would have experienced the same "economic miracle" without the model of and capital injection from Japan. However, as unpopular as it is to note in South Korea, Japan has had a lasting effect on South Korea's economic and business development.

Why did North Korea abduct Japanese citizens?

North Korea tragically abducted Japanese citizens in the late 1970s and early 1980s. It has forever and directly changed the lives of a number of Japanese citizens and their families. It has indirectly affected the lives of the entire Japanese nation. North Korean agents abducted seventeen Japanese nationals during this time frame, according to Japanese government authorities. Nongovernmental organizations cite a much larger number of missing persons cases that have gone unresolved as possible additional cases of North Korean abductions. The Japanese government has prioritized the abduction issue and established a special ministry to address it, but it has been unable to substantiate any claims beyond the official seventeen abductees.

The North Korean abductions are primarily tragic but also bizarre. It is hard to believe that a country would send its intelligence operatives to a foreign land to abduct a thirteen-year-old girl to get a Japanese language tutor to train its spies. Even in the late 1970s and early 1980s, one could think of a myriad of alternatives to learn Japanese: recruiting ethnic Koreans living in Japan with pro-DPRK sentiments as tutors, foreign-language immersions living undercover as South Korean nationals, or even books on tape. In fact, many Japanese remained skeptical that North Korea had abducted Japanese nationals for decades after the events. That is, until North Korean leader Kim Jong Il admitted it in 2002.

Japan's prime minister Junichiro Koizumi traveled to Pyongyang in 2002—and again in 2004—to meet Kim Jong Il. The only two Japan-DPRK summits to date focused on the abduction issue. In 2002, Kim admitted in writing that elements in his country had abducted Japanese nationals. Kim did not publicly disclose his country's motivation; he did not even officially accept responsibility for it. He did acknowledge that North Korean officials had carried out the abductions. Kim sought to avoid responsibility by suggesting he did not authorize the activity, and he never explicitly apologized for it. Nevertheless, Kim's admission was historic, and it put to rest debate on whether North Korea had ever abducted Japanese citizens. It had, and it returned at least some of them in exchange for economic and political concessions from Tokyo.

How has Japan tried to resolve the abduction issue?

Japanese prime minister Junichiro Koizumi visited Pyongyang twice. In 2002 and 2004, he met North Korean leader Kim Jong Il in Pyongyang for the only two Japan-DPRK summits in history. Koizumi focused on the abduction issue and gained concrete concessions in terms of people's lives. In September 2002, the two leaders signed the Pyongyang Declaration. In October 2002, Kim allowed five of the abductees to return home to Japan.[1] The two leaders agreed that the abductees' visit to Japan would be temporary, and that they would have to return to North Korea. However, Koizumi reneged on the agreement and kept the Japanese nationals. Kim responded by cutting off further talks.

Koizumi and his diplomats continued trying to secure the release of the remaining abductees. In 2004, Koizumi returned to Pyongyang for the second Japan-DPRK summit and secured the release of four children of Japanese abductees. North Korea calls the issue "resolved." Japan does not.

North Korea claims that the rest of the Japanese abductees are dead and they had provided their remains. Japan rejected the claim that the others were dead, and a Japanese DNA test seemed to show that the bones did not belong to the abducted individuals. Unfortunately, the validity of the scientific test itself was questionable, and the testing destroyed the sample, precluding further testing. There has been no credible proof that any of the abductees are alive, but the Japanese government operates from an assumption that they are. The North Koreans have periodically offered "re-investigations" into the issue in exchange for economic rewards, such as relief from certain Japanese sanctions.

What does North Korea want from Japan?

Japan is Korea's former colonial master, a critical ally of the United States, host to more US troops than any other country in the region (or the world), and North Korea's rich neighbor. Despite the complex relationship and web of North Korean demands on Japan that are possible, Pyongyang had primarily sought from Tokyo in recent years economic rewards.

Japan colonized Korea from 1910 to 1945. North Korean founder Kim Il Sung established his credentials as a military and political figure based on his experience fighting the Japanese imperial forces. The United States replaced Japan as North Korea's primary imperialist enemy after Japan's defeat in World War II. The United States supported Pyongyang's rival Korean government in Seoul and frustrated Kim Il

Sung's unification push during the Korean War. North Korea continues to criticize Japan's history of colonialism, especially on important anniversaries, but the United States took over as North Korea's leading concern in contemporary affairs. The colonial history does not dominate the bilateral North Korea–Japan relationship. Unlike the South Korea–Japan relationship, which has been marred by issues stemming from Japan's colonialism and World War II, including the Japanese military's abuse of Korean women during the conflict, the North Korea–Japan relationship has had its primary emphasis elsewhere.

Japan hosts approximately fifty thousand US troops on its territory, including the Third Marine Expeditionary Force and the Navy's Seventh Fleet. This mobile force is appropriately called the linchpin of the US security commitment to the entire region. United States Forces Japan would play an indispensable role in an American effort to defend South Korea in the event of another Korean War. North Korea would welcome a diminution of Japan's commitment to hosting the American forces as part of a broader effort to limit the US alliance framework around the Korean Peninsula; it has even noted that US troops in Japan are targets for its nuclear weapons. However, North Korea has not made Tokyo's hosting of US troops a top priority in its bilateral relationship with Japan. North Korea may see this as an implausible request or simply more distant from the more proximate North Korean security concern stemming from US troops in South Korea. Regardless of the motivation, North Korea's focus again is elsewhere.

North Korea wants money from Japan. Although China surpassed Japan as the world's second-largest economy in 2010, Japan is still the region's wealthiest country in many respects. Its people enjoy the highest standard of living and per capita GDP in Northeast Asia. North Korea wants to trade with Japan, and it wants economic aid.

In the short term, North Koreans would like to see Japan relax its unilateral sanctions on their country. Japanese consumers buy a lot of seafood, and North Korea used to be one of their suppliers. North Korea's exports were a tiny proportion of Japan's imports, but in the early 2000s, they made Japan North Korea's largest export destination after China. Pro–North Korea groups in Japan also used a ferry that operated between Japan and North Korea to send remittances back to North Korea. However, following North Korea's strategic provocations in its quest for nuclear-tipped ballistic missiles, Tokyo blocked bilateral trade, as well as the Japan–North Korea ferry operation.

In the longer term, North Korea also hopes that normalizing Japan–North Korea relations will yield an economic windfall. After Japan and South Korea established diplomatic relations in 1965, Tokyo provided Seoul with significant development aid that fueled South Korea's industrialization project. The two sides did not call the payments reparations for the colonial era, but the payments were intended to settle economic claims stemming from this time. Pyongyang expects that Tokyo will do the same if Japan establishes diplomatic relations with North Korea, too, and some have estimated a similar current-value sum amounting to about $10 billion. The CIA estimates North Korea's annual GDP at $40 billion, so this expectation if realized would be a major injection into the North Korean economy.

Tokyo has many outstanding issues with Pyongyang, including many of the same strategic issues that concern Seoul and Washington. But Tokyo also has a special interest in North Korea's abduction of Japanese citizens in the late 1970s and early 1980s. The two countries have negotiated the abduction issue and the return of the abductees in earnest since the early 2000s. North Korea claims it has returned all the living abductees, which Japan disputes. Continued differences between the two countries on this matter have been a major block to normalizing diplomatic relations.

Why did South Korea normalize diplomatic relations with Japan?

South Korean president Park Chung-hee established diplomatic relations with Japan in 1965. Though Japan remained unpopular in South Korea two decades after the end of its colonial rule, Park normalized the state-to-state relationship for geostrategic and economic reasons.

Park Chung-hee attended a Japanese military academy during the colonial period and served in the Japanese military during World War II as a colonial subject. Upon Korea's liberation, Park shifted to serve in the South Korean military, but the -die was already cast. The North Koreans and South Korean domestic critics charged that the South Korean leader was pro-Japanese. As a result, his decision to establish diplomatic relations with the country's former colonizer was not taken lightly.

Whether the South Koreans liked it or not, Japan was a significant player on the world stage and certainly in East Asia. South Koreans speak today about the four great powers most central to its national interests—the United States, Russia, China, and Japan. Seeking to ignore Japan in international politics handicapped South Korea, and establishing diplomatic relations with Tokyo allowed Seoul to engage the larger Japan on a range of critical matters of state.

Japan was also a US treaty ally. In the 1960s, South Korea was dependent on the United States for security and economic support. It was no secret that Washington then—as now—wanted to see better relations between Seoul and Tokyo. Establishing diplomatic relations would be the most significant step in building this relationship since Korea's liberation in 1945.

Park also sought to develop South Korea's economy. Japan was and is South Korea's richer neighbor. Normalizing relations sought to address long-standing economic issues stemming from the colonial era and World War II. Japan would not pay "reparations" for the war, but normalization came with a large Japanese development commitment to address the past. Park used the Japanese capital to feed his ambitious economic development project. South Korea's economic miracle is a credit to the hard work of the Korean people, smart developmental policy by the Park government, and critical injections of foreign capital from the United States and Japan.

Park was a political leader who came to power by coup and grew more authoritarian later in his reign. Nonetheless, he took the domestic political risk and made the unpopular decision to reconcile with Japan. When his daughter successfully ran for president in 2012, her father's decision to normalize relations with Japan in 1965 would still be used as political ammunition to criticize her for being too pro-Japan. When she attempted to raise historical issues related to Japan's sexual abuse of Korean women during World War II, her father's legacy became even more pronounced and made it politically more difficult for her to reach accommodation with Tokyo. Nevertheless, Park Chung-hee's legitimacy and legacy stems from his transforming South Korea from a poor agricultural state to a rapidly industrializing one, and his decision to normalize relations with Japan advanced that agenda.

What are the historical and territorial issues in South Korea–Japan relations?

The Japanese and Korean people have inhabited their respective lands in the form of various centralized dynasties, feudal groupings of localities, and strong and weak governments for millennia. Koreans point to pirates operating out of Japan as early forms of Japanese invasions of Korea. The Japanese point to continental Asian security threats, primarily from China, crossing the Korean Peninsula like a dagger directed at the heart of Japan, as demonstrating the inherent relevance of Korean politics to Japanese security. However interesting the deeper history may be, the main historical issues that animate South Korea–Japan disagreements today are rooted in the 1910–1945 Japanese colonization of Korea.

Korean strategists and politicians note a worry about a revival of Japanese militarism. After Japan's late nineteenth-century interaction with Western imperialism, Japan quickly and radically revolutionized its society, polity, and military within a few short decades. Japan went from being a victim of Western imperialism to an emulator of it. Japan joined the ranks of great powers vying for foreign influence, especially over Korea, and won in a succession of quick wars with China and Russia. Japan annexed Korea in 1910 as its military power continued to develop. Although they recognize that Japan's pacifist tradition and constitution has meant Japan has not carried out anything like this since 1945, some Koreans worry that a revival of Japanese militarism could again be devastating if those legal restrictions or norms erode.

Japan's pacifist constitution was a product of a defeated power. At the conclusion of World War II, the Emperor of Japan accepted unconditional surrender, and the American military occupied the country. The United States—and the war-exhausted Japanese society—had no interest in seeing a revival of Japanese militarism. The Japanese constitution legally prohibited the country from offensively waging war, and its Self Defense Force remains today heavily circumscribed by legal and constitutional prohibitions in exercising force. Ironically, the foreign power most responsible for Japan's pacifist constitution, the United States, is now also the power most likely to support its loosened interpretation or even revision. The United States tends to support Japan's taking on additional roles in providing its own defense to lessen the US military burden, as well as contribute to regional stability.

Koreans are generally less convinced that Japan's moves away from militarism after 1945 are permanent and irreversible, recalling how quickly and devastatingly the government, society, and military shifted to aggression in the late nineteenth century through the first half of the twentieth century. Further, the lessons young Japanese learn about the past and the understanding its current leaders have about it are relevant. The controversial museum at Japan's Yasukuni Shrine recounts a right-wing Japanese narrative about World War II. The museum explains that US sanctions on Japan forced the strike on Pearl Harbor, fails to mention that Japanese human rights abuses were outside the norms of war, laments the decision to surrender even after the atomic bombings, and rejects the legitimacy of the Tokyo Trials against Japanese war criminals. The narrative portrays Japan as a victim rather than a responsible party that must learn from past mistakes. As such, Koreans, among others, take umbrage at the conservative Japanese politicians who visit the shrine. Even though these Japanese politicians generally do not visit the museum and note that their visits merely honor the country's war dead, which some Japanese politicians have justified as analogous to an American president's visit to Arlington National Cemetery, the visits are intimately tied to the controversial elements of the Shinto Shrine's right-wing past and message. For the Koreans, this is a dangerous failure to come to terms with history, learn from it, and ensure that it does not repeat.

In a similar way, Korean officials have objected to Japanese textbooks that fail to recognize Japan's aggression in the past. On a more personal level, Koreans often find it insulting when Japanese politicians fail to recognize their military's actions in World War II that forced women, primarily Koreans and Chinese, into brothels to service Japanese soldiers. Japanese politicians who claim that these victims, dubbed "comfort women," had voluntarily signed up to be prostitutes stir up particular resentment. In 1993, Japanese Chief Cabinet Secretary Yohei Kono extended the Government of Japan's "sincere apologies and remorse" for all those who suffered as comfort women, and subsequent Japanese leaders have referred to the statement.[2] However, Japanese politicians' refusal to periodically repeat the words of the Japanese apology became a years-long diplomatic dispute. Even moderate Japanese will ask how many times their government must apologize for the past, whereas Koreans see the issue as a living history that must be actively remembered. South Korean groups have erected statues to these "comfort women," as the aging and shrinking group of survivors is called, in various locations, including in front of Japanese diplomatic facilities. Tokyo has strongly protested the statues.

Japan–South Korea territorial issues are likewise rooted in a contentious history. A set of small islands that Koreans call Dokdo and Japanese call Takeshima is in the body of water between the two countries. Both claim the land as their own. A South Korean couple permanently resides on Dokdo, and rotating South Korean coast guard and administrative personnel also live there, precluding any claim that the small islands are uninhabited. Nevertheless, the islands' material and geopolitical significance is far less than the amount of political attention the two sides have placed on the small land formations. Japan first claimed the islets as its own in 1905—just five years before annexing all of Korea, so the sovereignty dispute is critically linked to the broader question of Japanese colonialism and the competing nationalisms between the two countries.

What are the common strategic interests in South Korea–Japan relations?

South Korea and Japan share their most important ally, the United States, and most acute national security threat, North Korea. Both also maintain an uneasy relationship with China, but Japan is more explicit that it sees China as a rival. The two countries are capitalist, industrialized democracies and share foundational political values. South Korean and Japanese strategic interests are highly aligned even if competing nationalisms and identity politics drive them apart.

South Korea and Japan both allow tens of thousands of American troops to station themselves permanently on their soil. Japan is the single largest host nation of American troops; approximately fifty thousand American service personnel live and work in the country. South Korea is not far behind, hosting almost 28,500 American service personnel. For Washington, its allies in Tokyo and Seoul are its most important in the region. South Korea relies on the United States to augment its own significant military to deter and, if necessary, defend against North Korean aggression. The US–Japan alliance is more regionally focused and mobile, defending Japanese territory and preserving regional security from emerging threats, including but not limited to North Korea. Unlike in South Korea, the US military presence in Japan does not augment a robust Japanese fighting force but helps to assuage foreign concerns about Japanese remilitarization by helping Japan defend itself without maintaining a larger standing fighting force of its own.

As long-standing allies of the United States, Seoul and Tokyo are both encouraged by Washington to support similar initiatives. Since both states are advanced capitalist trading states and democracies, they share many of the same values that motivate these initiatives in the first place. For example, the economies of South Korea and Japan depend critically on the free flow of commerce through the South China Sea. The energy-starved countries import oil from the Middle East that traverses these sea lanes, and any closure of that trade could grind both economies to a halt. Both countries have a natural interest in supporting freedom of navigation in international waters. Likewise, the two democracies regularly support and fund human rights initiatives in third countries and invest in the sustainable development of poorer countries in a way consistent with these democratic values.

South Korea and Japan also fundamentally agree on the challenge posed by North Korea. Though South Korean presidential administrations oscillate in their preferred approaches to inter-Korean economic projects and political engagement, they retain universal male conscription and a large standing army oriented to defending against one overriding security threat: North Korea. South Korean leaders may smile for the cameras with North Korean leaders at summits, speak about pan-Korean nationalism, and even supply aid to their northern "brothers." However, none has radically reduced the potency of the South Korean fighting force to stand ready, along with the United States, to "fight tonight" (one of the mottos of the US–ROK combined force) and repulse North Korean aggression.

Japan is not part of the divided Korean nation, so it does not face the complexities of identity politics that South Korea does. Japanese leaders can more simply look to stand up to the North Korean threat. Japan regularly seeks to enhance military planning with the United States and South Korea given the common security threat. Tokyo understands that Washington's troops on its soil would be critically involved in responding to any North Korean contingency. American forces in South Korea are on the front lines, but US troops in Japan are not far behind. Japan would supply much of the rear area support, such as large field hospitals and transportation hubs, in the event of war in Korea. The US, South Korean, and Japanese military planners in particular are aligned, as one can imagine, on the North Korean threat even as politics and contentious issues in the South Korean–Japanese historical relationship makes cooperation more difficult.

Japan and South Korea also are suspicious of China's intentions as it continues to rise and expand its military capabilities and reach. Japan is more explicit about its rivalry with China, whereas South Korea tries to avoid antagonizing its western neighbor too much. Japan and South Korea each claim China as its largest trading partner. However, Japan is a larger economy and the country and has the greater wherewithal to stand up to the Chinese. Beijing can and has bullied Seoul with its economic leverage. For example, after South Korea agreed to host a US missile defense site targeted at North Korean missiles, China worried that the technology could nullify its own missile capabilities. Beijing strongly objected and targeted South Korean firms operating in China. Given the two countries' disparate economic power, the trade measures hurt South Korea deeply and ultimately prompted the South Korean government to stop adding to the missile defense site as previously planned. Japan is also subject to Chinese economic pressure, but with an economy five times larger than South Korea's, Tokyo has greater power and resolve to resist.

6

US–SOUTH KOREA RELATIONS
IN THE TWENTY-FIRST
CENTURY

How do South Koreans see the United States today?

South Koreans overwhelmingly see the United States, the US–South Korea alliance, and the American people, positively. The Pew Research Center showed South Koreans had a more positive view of the "American people" than any other country polled, with 86 percent seeing Americans favorably. South Koreans vary their support for "the United States," including governmental policy, depending on the occupant of the White House. South Korea approval of the United States peaked at 84 percent in 2015, the last year of the Obama administration, when 88 percent of South Koreans registered positive feelings toward Obama. This dropped to 75 percent of South Koreans seeing "the United States" favorably in 2017 under the Trump administration because only 17 percent of South Koreans liked Trump.[1] South Korean public opinion can shift quickly and radically, especially when tragic events involving the US military presence in South Korea combine with nationalism, but high support rates have returned over time.

Though South Korean public opinion can oscillate widely, relative support rates by generation are incredibly stable. It is not a simple story of people growing more conservative as they age. South Korea's oldest generation is the most conservative and supports the United States most strongly, the youngest generation is moderate, and the middle generation is the most critical. The oldest generation of South Koreans, with the closest experiences with the Korean War and American support in repulsing the North Korean invasion, has the most positive view of the United States. The "386 generation" refers to Koreans who were in their thirties when the term was coined in the 1990s (when the 386 computer chip was the state of the art), politically active in the 1980s democratization movement, and born in the 1960s. This generation contrasted with their parents in criticizing the United States, seeking peaceful accommodation with North Korea over competition, and placing more emphasis on national sovereignty. The youngest generation is somewhere in the middle and has the most global outlook.

In the South Korean authoritarian era, public opinion did not have the same role public opinion has under democracy. South Koreans appeared to support the United States as their defender against a repeat of North Korea's invasion of South Korea that devastated the peninsula. The MacArthur statue in Incheon commemorates the American general's landing there that changed the tide of the Korean War. Its effusive praise for MacArthur reflects some of the intensely pro-American views of South Korea's oldest generation and explains their children's reaction against it. It is common to find older Koreans in downtown Seoul waving American flags or public exhibits voicing appreciation for the contributions of the American and UN forces to South Korean security during the Korean War and beyond.

South Korea's democratization movement created space for a greater diversity of views. The 1980 Gwangju incident gave birth to wider South Korean criticism of the United States. As young South Koreans increasingly demanded political rights, large-scale protests spread across the country. In that progressive stronghold in southwest Korea, the South Korean military government violently suppressed a protest.

The victims believed that the United States was behind or at least supported the military government's bloody crackdown. They would grow more skeptical of the United States as a beacon of democracy and human rights as they saw the United States standing behind the South Korean authoritarian government despite its resistance to democratization. The United States advocated human rights in South Korea in many ways, but its effectiveness was open to debate, and South Korea's progressives became much more deeply critical of the US role in South Korea and its military presence as an affront to sovereignty.

The US military presence in Korea has been a lightning rod for criticism. When American soldiers committed horrendous crimes, the criminal matter often became political. Traffic accidents involving American military vehicles that tragically killed Korean schoolchildren likewise produced mass protests. Beyond the US military presence, trade disputes also stimulated protest against the United States. In 2008, a US–South Korea agreement to allow the resumption of American beef exports to Korea despite food-safety allegations led to the largest protests in Korea since the 1980s democratization movement. Much of Korean society thought the beef was unsafe, and that their government was bowing to the Americans as their political lackey. Washington was disregarding the health and safety of the Korean people to pad its businesses' bottom line, they argued. After these significant swings in Korean public opinion of the United States, high approval rates for the United States returned.

What is the US military presence in South Korea?

The United States has maintained a permanent military presence in South Korea since World War II.[2] US Forces Korea has as its mission to deter and, if necessary, defend against North Korean aggression. After World War II, the allies that had defeated Japan, namely, the United States and the Soviet

Union, occupied Japan's former colony. The Soviets occupied the northern portion of the Korean Peninsula, and Americans the southern part. Specifically, in the south, Washington supported a provisional Korean government until the Republic of Korea was declared in 1948. The US military was demobilizing after World War II, returning American soldiers home to civilian life. Its main concern in the Pacific during World War II was Japan, and the bulk of American forces in the region remained there to try to make sure Japan did not re-emerge as threat to American interests and regional stability.

North Korea's invasion of South Korea on June 25, 1950, invigorated the American defense establishment to act against a perceived expansion of global communism. North Korea nearly pushed the US and South Korean forces off the peninsula in the summer of 1950. Although Korea was a relatively low priority for the United States in the late 1940s, when Washington was focused on crafting a new international order, the Korean War and Cold War preoccupation with communism as a global threat refocused American attention on Korea.

After the Korean War ground to a stalemate in 1953, the United States and South Korea signed a mutual defense treaty. US forces would defend South Korea and constrain its virulently anticommunist president Syngman Rhee from restarting the Korean War in his own bid to reunify the country. Even as North Korean leader Kim Il Sung demanded that Chinese forces depart from North Korean territory, an exit that was completed in 1958, South Korea consented to a permanent US military presence on its soil.

The US military presence in South Korea has served as the first US defense against North Korea, as well as a tripwire guaranteeing that more American troops would flow to South Korea in event of another Korean War. The ability of the United States to defend South Korea robustly—and to effectively communicate this to North Korea—has been important in preserving the peace since 1953. North Korea may have believed at various times in its history that it could defeat the South Korean military, but it knew it was no match for the combined US–South Korea force. The threat of retaliation from the United States has deterred North Korea from initiating general war on the peninsula since 1953.

The size of the US troop presence in South Korea has changed over the decades. As the American populace and government grew more opposed to military deployments in Asia during the Vietnam War, the United States in 1971 shrank the number of American troops in Korea by one-third. Washington stressed that its nuclear umbrella against Soviet or Chinese support for a potential North Korean invasion remained firmly in place, while it encouraged greater South Korean "burden-sharing." In other words, South Korea would need to do more to provide for its own defense. The United States in the late 1970s even seriously discussed the complete withdrawal of US forces from Korea, despite Seoul's deep concern and opposition. Washington objected to the authoritarian South Korean government's human rights abuses, and Seoul worried that losing the US deterrent would invite Pyongyang to invade again. However, Washington never implemented this complete-withdrawal proposal. Later technological developments in military affairs and US military commitments elsewhere, including in Iraq, led to further reductions in US forces in South Korea.

The United States' military presence in South Korea has shrunk to the current levels of around 28,500 US troops. As the US military footprint shrank, military needs evolved, and South Korean cities grew to make certain bases like the Yongsan Garrison headquarters in Seoul effectively in the middle of the South Korean capital, the two allies agreed to close a variety of US bases in South Korea and consolidate them. The military and geopolitical significance of the US force has remained the same over the decades but the specific size and basing structure of the US military footprint has evolved.

What are the US–South Korea military exercises?

In peacetime, professional militaries prepare for war. They develop strategies and specific plans to conduct war in case national political leaders call upon them to do so. Militaries practice those plans in various ways to make sure strategies worked out on paper can actually be implemented—or have at least been thought through—on the battlefield. Military exercises are that practice.

North Korea strenuously objects to US–South Korean military exercises. They call them war rehearsals. They assert that these are practice offensive attacks on North Korea, and point to some controversial exercises such as "decapitation strikes" that rehearse destroying North Korean leadership targets. In contrast, the United States and South Korea emphasize that the drills are defensive. They are not training for an invasion but for how to respond if North Korea strikes first. North Korea has not been reassured.

Pyongyang also complains that the exercises bring a large number of US troops and sophisticated military equipment to the Korean theater. If the United States intended to invade North Korea, bringing additional troops and nuclear-capable assets to the region under the auspices of a peaceful drill would position it perfectly to launch a surprise attack, the North says. As a result, North Korea responds to the drills with its own military mobilization. It assumes the exercises might be preemptive attacks and goes on alert. This drains the country's military of scarce resources like fuel and generally irritates Pyongyang.

North Korea has long called for the suspension and cancellation of exercises. China strongly supports this demand, fearing itself the introduction of American aircraft carrier strike groups and strategic bombers into its backyard. Following the US–North Korea summit of June 12, 2018, President Trump agreed to suspend the next major US–South Korea military exercise, previously scheduled for that August. The move was intended to address North Korea's long-held security concern and to be a confidence-building measure to encourage North Korea to step away from its nuclear weapons. Trump's concession was not the first time this quid pro quo had been executed; the United States had canceled its much larger Team Spirit exercise to gain North Korean denuclearization commitments in the 1994 Agreed Framework as well.

What are contemporary issues in the US–South Korea military alliance?

As allies with significant regional and global roles, the United States and South Korea approach together a worldwide set of priorities with the North Korea issue consistently topping the list. Matters specifically pertaining to the bilateral military alliance, however, focus often on questions surrounding the basing of US troops, national authorities to command the two countries' troops, and procurement and development of military hardware.

US troops reside in South Korea at the invitation of the South Korean government and with the consent of US political authorities. As guests in South Korea, the US military makes significant efforts to ensure they remain good neighbors. However, when American troops commit crimes, the US military and South Korean authorities determine jurisdiction according to a status of forces agreement (SOFA) and prosecute the crimes accordingly. Questions of proper jurisdiction and whether the American or South Korean authorities will prosecute can become political matters when US soldiers based in South Korea commit heinous crimes or tragic accidents occur. Responding to "incidents and accidents" is a constant duty in alliance management related to the basing of US troops in South Korea.

Where and how US troops are stationed is another mainstay of alliance management. For example, the headquarters of US Forces Korea is in the Yongsan Garrison. Once on the outskirts of Seoul, the Yongsan Garrison has seen the expansion of the South Korean capital around it for decades in such a way that the base now sits on valuable real estate near the center of the city. The two sides have been negotiating, planning, and executing the downsizing and eventual closure of the base for years. The US military has been gradually moving more people and functions to a large base in rural South Korea, farther from possible North Korean barrages, and allowing the return of valuable real estate to South Korea. In exchange, South Korea is paying for most of the move.

The United States and South Korea both benefit from the alliance relationship and basing US troops there. Determining which nation's taxpayers fund it is thus a constant issue. The two countries split the cost, but what the levels of funding will be, and the particulars of what is funded, is a multibillion-dollar question, negotiated with a fine-tooth comb.

The South Korean alliance is a combined force. This means that the two militaries are formally integrated. The commander of the combined forces is an American four-star general, and his deputy is a South Korean four-star general. South Korean soldiers serve on the security detail of the US commander and the two sides look to integrate at every level of military organization below this top level as much as possible. The US–South Korea alliance is not a "joint" force operating in parallel toward common objectives, but a "combined" force seeking to fuse separate militaries into a single fighting force to the greatest extent possible.

The four-star American general in South Korea wears many hats. He is the Commander of US Forces Korea, the US–South Korean Combined Forces, and the UN Command. In wartime, the US general has command authority to direct both the US and South Korean forces in battle. Some South Koreans have opposed this arrangement as a violation of South Korean sovereignty, but South Korean generals have been the most outspoken in the arrangement's defense. They note that the command relationship that would be triggered in the case of another war on the peninsula keeps the United States engaged and, critically, helps South Korea defend itself. A South Korean general commands South Korean troops in all other situations. The two sides agreed to shift wartime operational control back to South Korea when its military is able to defend the country under this command arrangement. The agreement is vague and ensures future discussions on whether the South Korean military can meet this metric.[3]

Last but not least, the US–South Korean combined force must develop or buy expensive military hardware. Naturally, Washington would prefer that Seoul buy American. It helps make sure the two militaries' equipment can operate well together in wartime and supports the US defense industry. South Korea's lawmakers and taxpayers value having an interoperable combined force and the proper stewardship of its defense budget. In other words, there may be an instinctive preference for American military goods, but price matters too. South Korea's development of its own defense industry is another consideration for Seoul.

The acquisition or development of South Korean defense assets covers many areas, but the highest profile issue in recent years has been missile defense. Seoul initially decided to develop its own missile defense system that would run in parallel to the American regionally based defense, rather than directly be integrated into it. South Korean leaders hoped this move would give South Korea greater autonomy from the United States on these defense issues; allow it to keep its distance from the other major participant in the American missile defense arrangement, Japan; and avoid estranging South Korea's top trading partner, China.[4] At the same time, the decision created alliance challenges that had to be actively managed to ensure that the new South Korean system really could integrate with US missile defense assets to guard against common North Korea missile threats. South Korea's decision in 2016 to base advanced US missile defense batteries called THAAD on its territory augmented this regional defense but embroiled it in a diplomatic and economic spat with China that convinced Seoul to halt further expansions of the THAAD system on their soil.[5]

What are contemporary issues in the US–South Korea trade relationship?

After many years of negotiations, the US–Korea Free Trade Agreement (KORUS FTA) came into effect in 2012. The agreement sought to reduce barriers to trade between the largest economy in the world (the United States) and the twelfth largest (South Korea). The United States is also South Korea's second largest trade partner (after China), and South Korea is the United States' sixth largest trading partner (after China, Canada, Mexico, Japan, and Germany). The KORUS FTA was the most important US trade deal since the North American Free Trade Agreement (NAFTA) that had come into force eighteen years earlier.

Trade deals quickly get very detailed as industries on both sides press their governments to secure every trade advantage possible. A persistent issue in US–South Korea trade negotiations surrounds automobiles. Korean cars made by Hyundai and KIA are common on American roads, but American car brands are a rare sight in Korea. Before the ratification of the KORUS FTA, South Korea exported about five hundred thousand autos to the United States. The United States exported only 7,500 to South Korea. Although consumer preference plays a role, the striking disparity underlined some governmental protection of Korea's automobile industry, American negotiators and industry representatives noted.

South Korea imposed a number of rules and regulations on autos before they could be sold in their country. For example, they required a higher safety standard be met than the American regulations demanded, which American carmakers argued was unnecessary and made it harder for them to sell cars in South Korea. It is expensive for American automakers to tailor their manufacturing to the relatively small South

Korean market, and they charged that the safety regulations were just a cover meant to limit American penetration in the South Korean market. In a compromise, the KORUS FTA allowed each American carmaker to sell up to 25,000 vehicles in South Korea that met only the US safety standard.[6]

Beef had also been a prime area of trade disputes ahead of the KORUS FTA. After Mad Cow disease was found in a single cow in the United States in 2003, South Korea joined several other countries in banning American beef imports, citing food-safety concerns. The United States charged the blanket ban was unwarranted, and key members of Congress from the cattle-raising states made sure the US administration did not sidestep the issue. American cattle ranchers wanted to sell to the fifty million South Koreans.

In 2008, South Korean president Lee Myung-bak lifted the US beef ban, which led some Koreans to conclude that their democratically elected government was toeing the line for the American ally instead of representing the health interests of Koreans. They turned out in the streets in the largest protests in South Korea since the democratization movement in the 1980s. The issue at hand was at least as much about nationalism and sovereignty as trade policy and health. After additional negotiations, US beef exports to South Korea have normalized, and Korean consumers appear mostly comfortable with the safety of the American product as judged by the renewed US dominance of the Korean beef market.

Donald Trump criticized a variety of American trade deals during the 2016 presidential campaign. After his inauguration in 2017, he withdrew from some trade deals, such as the Trans-Pacific Partnership, and sought to renegotiate others, such as the KORUS FTA. America's trade partners almost universally resisted, but South Korea agreed to an abbreviated trade negotiation as part of a broader effort to keep the United States and South Korea aligned as North Korea–related diplomacy heated up.

In 2018, the two allies reached a quick agreement that modified the trade pact. The trade imbalance on autos remained considerable. South Korean agreed to double the quota on each American automaker's exports to South Korea using American safety standards. Instead of being allowed to export twenty-five thousand vehicles to South Korea at the American safety standard, each American carmaker now could export fifty thousand vehicles. In exchange, South Korea would enjoy a quicker phase-out of American tariffs on South Korean pick-up trucks. However, no American carmaker had come close to the twenty-five-thousand mark, so doubling the quota had no immediate effect. Also, no South Korean auto company exported any pick-up trucks to the United States, so as many economists noted, this provision, too, would have little to no effect. South Korea also agreed to limit the quantity of steel it exported to the United States, and South Korea would not be subject to American steel tariffs in return.[7]

7

KOREAN LEADERSHIP IN THE TWENTY-FIRST CENTURY

What were the ten years of progressive rule in South Korea?

After South Korea's democratization in the late 1980s, the country continued to be led by conservative presidents until the South Korean populace elected progressive candidate Kim Dae-jung in 1997; he was inaugurated the following year. South Korean presidents serve a five-year term and cannot be re-elected. Kim Dae-jung's successor was another progressive, Roh Moo-hyun. The period when the two presidents held office were the ten years of progressive rule in South Korea, which lasted from 1998 to 2008.

South Korean progressives and conservatives differ on some domestic political priorities, but the most striking policy departure concerns North Korea. South Korean president Kim Dae-jung sought to revolutionize the inter-Korean relationship with his Sunshine Policy. Named after an Aesop fable that taught that the sun's warmth rather than the wind's cold encouraged a man to remove his coat, the Sunshine Policy sought to modify North Korean behavior with warmth. Kim Dae-jung's Sunshine Policy wanted to transform the confrontation with North Korea to economic cooperation and political accommodation.

Kim Dae-jung's administration reached out to North Korea, and leaders of the two Koreas agreed to meet on June 15, 2000.

It would be the first ever inter-Korean summit, and Kim Dae-jung traveled to Pyongyang for it. The summit touched off a long and uneven path toward what Kim Dae-jung hoped would be reconciliation and eventual unification. South Korea would invest in a business park in North Korea, replete with South Korean managers and North Korean labor. The two countries would cooperate on a tourism project at North Korea's Mount Kumgang that welcomed South Korean tourists before its closure. Seoul provided aid, ostensibly to help the North Korean people, but it was critically short on monitoring protocols to avoid the diversion of aid, putting South Korea's aid practices outside the international standard. Inter-Korean relations thawed, but Pyongyang showed no signs of letting up on its aggressive military posture and nuclear development. When Kim Dae-jung's term ended, another South Korean progressive, Roh Moo-hyun, continued the same broad contours of his predecessor's Sunshine Policy under a different name.

The US–South Korean relationship suffered during South Korea's ten years of progressive rule. Progressive Kim Dae-jung and his American contemporary, President George W. Bush, had different approaches to North Korea policy. The two leaders got off to a rocky start as Kim tried to convince Bush of his vision for engaging North Korea, to no avail. The two allies managed disagreements to try to preserve a united front at the nascent Six Party Talks on North Korean denuclearization. However, South Korea's election of a more ideological progressive president, Roh Moon-hyun (2003–2008), led to an even more tense period in the US–South Korea alliance.

Roh Moo-hyun ruled a divided administration, and certain senior officials in his camp were openly anti-American. They emphasized Korean sovereignty from a nationalistic lens and seemed to some Americans to degrade the value of the alliance and nature of the long-held American security commitment to South Korea. Roh's administration included members of the 386 generation, who equated the United States with South Korean conservative administrations, including its authoritarian-era presidents and their human rights abuses. The Roh government grew closer to China, and the South Korea population grew increasingly disenchanted with Roh over his perceived failures on the economy as well as the worsening US–South Korean relationship.[1]

South Korean conservatives lamented the ten years of progressive rule and labeled Kim and Roh dangerously naïve. They highlighted revelations that Kim Dae-jung arranged a $500 million payment to North Korea to secure the first inter-Korean summit as evidence of an insincere giveaway policy. Critics called South Korea's aid wasted, as North Korea never moderated its security threat to the South. The 2008 election year favored South Korean conservatives, and the country elected conservative Lee Myung-bak. Lee promised economic revitalization, a reinvigorated US–South Korea alliance, and a harder line on North Korea.

What was the South Korean conservative response to the ten years of progressive rule?

The ten years of progressive rule experimented with crafting a new inter-Korean relationship. However, South Korean voters grew impatient with promises of a return on that investment. In 2007, they elected a conservative to the Blue House, and inter-Korean policy turned back toward conditioning aid and trade on North Korea's denuclearization and improvement in the security relationship.

Inter-Korean projects had some staying power initially, but they eventually closed down after this initial progressive era in South Korean politics ended. After a North Korean guard in 2008 shot and killed a South Korean tourist who had ventured into a restricted portion of a beach near the Mount Kumgang resort, Seoul demanded an apology and investigation. North Korea was not ready to meet that demand. Seoul pulled the plug on the project. After a South Korean report with international participants concluded that in 2010 North Korea had torpedoed a South Korean naval vessel, the *Cheonan*, South Korea imposed unilateral sanctions on all economic exchanges with North Korea outside the Kaesong Industrial Complex. Further North Korean provocations would prompt Seoul to close the complex later.

South Korea inaugurated another conservative president in 2013, Park Geun-hye, who defined her North Korea policy as "trust-building" and gave a major address in Dresden, Germany, in 2014, outlining her unification vision. Pyongyang voiced no interest in her proposal and openly worried that the speech's location in Germany suggested that Park was interested in unification by absorption on the German model. Unable to gain traction with the North Koreans, Park pursued a more reactive policy, as she urged imposing more economic sanctions on the North at the UN Security Council and military deterrence with the United States in response to continued North Korean missile and nuclear demonstrations.

However, Park Geun-hye's largest legacy as it relates to North Korea policy is the effect her 2017 impeachment and 2018 removal from office had on paving the way for progressive president Moon Jae-in. In April 2014, an overfilled South Korean ferry traveling to the South Korean Jeju island sank, killing 304 people on-board, including 250 high school students. Park's approval rating slipped amid her government's response. Park had a more reserved persona and failed to shine as consoler-in-chief. Her ruling style of limiting public and even elite access to her, however, would prove her ultimate undoing.

In 2016, it became clear that Park's long-time confidante, Choi Soon-sil, had outsized influence on the president. Choi was a cult leader, not a well-known and respected adviser. She pressured large South Korean conglomerates to donate millions of dollars to organizations she controlled in exchange for representing the conglomerates' interests with Park. Nationwide protests swelled; Park's approval rating dropped to single digits; and the National Assembly voted to impeach her in December 2016. South Korea's high court upheld the impeachment in March 2017, and extreme popular dissatisfaction with the conservative incumbent paved the way for progressive candidate Moon Jae-in to win the presidency. Moon would take a decidedly different approach to North Korean diplomacy.

Who is North Korean leader Kim Jong Un?

Kim Jong Un holds many titles, but his status as the undisputed top leader of North Korea stems from his bloodline rather than these positions. His grandfather, Kim Il Sung, was founder of North Korea. Kim Il Sung bequeathed his kingdom to his eldest son, Kim Jong Il. Kim Jong Il, in turn, groomed his third son as his own successor, and Kim Jong Un took over ruling the country in December 2011, upon Kim Jong Il's death.

Kim Jong Un grew up in privilege. He attended boarding school in Switzerland under an alias. As Kim Jong Il's third son, he was not the natural pick to succeed his father. However, Kim Jong Un's elder half-brother, Kim Jong Nam, fell out of favor with their father in the late 1990s. The precise reasons for Kim Jong Nam's fall cannot be firmly identified, but he did seem to prefer more rapid economic reform than his father. Kim Jong Un's mother, who was not the biological mother of Kim Jong Nam, also advocated for her son to rule. Kim Jong Nam also attempted to visit Tokyo Disneyland on a fake passport in 2001 and embarrassed the family when Japanese authorities caught him. Kim Jong Nam lived in exile in Macau and Beijing under assumed Chinese protection. After Kim Jong Un's rise to power, North Korean agents orchestrated Kim Jong Nam's gruesome assassination using VX nerve agent when Kim Jong Nam was outside China at a Malaysian airport.

Kim Jong Un's other older brother, Kim Jong Chol, never appeared under consideration for the top political job in North Korea. Although he was Kim Jong Un's only full brother born of the same mother, Kim Jong Il considered Kim Jong Chol too effeminate for the dictatorial responsibilities, according to the family's former sushi chef. After Kim Jong Il suffered a near-fatal stroke in August 2008, he accelerated succession preparations for his third son, Kim Jong Un. Upon Kim Jong Il's death in December 2011, Kim Jong Un ruled the country.

Many foreign observers doubted whether the twenty-eight- or twenty-nine-year old could really run the North Korean system. Some believed Kim Jong Un's powerful aunt or uncle would run the country in all but name. As Kim Jong Un took on more titles as leader of North Korea's main political institutions and grew more accustomed to the functions of power, he dramatically demonstrated that he was in charge. In 2013, Kim Jong Un publicly tried and executed his once-powerful uncle, Jang Song Thaek.

Kim Jong Un had inherited the reins of power from his father, but he decided to emulate his grandfather. North Korean founder Kim Il Sung was a charismatic leader, a self-made man respected for his anti-Japanese guerilla roots, and the leader of North Korea during its ascent. Kim Jong Il, by contrast, was an introverted micromanager; the privileged son of the leader, passionate about art and cinema; and leader of North Korea during its decline. Kim Jong Un restored the annual New Year's Day address, convened long-defunct party congresses, and showcased the first family. Kim Jong Un was a reformer in the sense that he departed from his father's style of rule, but he was not a closet capitalist or aspiring democrat. He sought to leverage nostalgia and return to the authoritarian practices more common in the North Korean heyday.

Nevertheless, Kim Jong Un was not a revolutionary, and many of the attributes of North Korea common to both his grandfather and father remain the same today. Human rights abuses remain rampant, including the employment of a network of prison camps. Despite increasing roles for markets and economic incentives, the economy remains overwhelmingly directed at the commanding heights by the state. The Kim regime continues to elicit loyalty from the ruling class and masses by approaching everything from housing to educational and medical access to wages and jobs based on perceived loyalty to the regime. The cult of personality and propaganda machine supporting it continues to imbue the Kim family with superhuman abilities. Hatred for the United States and the development of nuclear aspirations continue. Kim Jong Un has notable differences from his father, but he remains at his core the leader of the same North Korean regime.

What happened when Kim Jong Il died?

Kim Jong Il died on December 14, 2011. When the regime announced his death three days later, it caught the world by surprise. To the embarrassment of South Korean intelligence, North Korea kept the secret hidden even while preparing an orderly and elaborate structured outpouring of grief for the late leader.

For years, North Korea watchers debated expectations for this third generation succession. Kim Il Sung tapped Kim Jong Il as his successor in 1980 and gradually shifted power to him before the older Kim's death in 1994. Though analysts debate precisely when Kim Jong Il first tapped Kim Jong Un to succeed him, the succession accelerated after Kim Jong Il's 2008 stroke. In all of the assumptions about the specific time frame for Kim Jong Un's succession, there is wide agreement that Kim Jong Un had only a few years of grooming before taking the top post.

Kim Jong Il's death marked the most substantial leadership challenge in North Korea in a generation, yet it progressed without outward signs of political instability or widespread internal strife. Kim Jong Un moved to install his own loyalists and purged senior officials, including executing his own uncle, but he maintained control over the regime throughout. The succession proceeded smoothly with significant leadership purges well within the standard North Korean playbook. In short, Kim Jong Il's death replaced one Kim at the top of North Korean politics with another.

Why did Kim Jong Un execute his uncle?

In 2013, North Korean authorities charged Kim Jong Un's uncle, Jang Song Thaek, with factionalist subversion of the state. Factionalism was a charge utilized since the 1940s and widely employed in the 1950s to eliminate any individual perceived as disloyal or potentially disloyal to the Kim rule. The charge publicly detailed Jang's apparent corruption and suggested a perceived threat to Kim Jong Un's rule. A three-man military tribunal quickly convicted Jang on the capital charges, and he was executed. A man once deemed the second most powerful individual in the country was now dead.

Jang likely was corrupt and did use his office and family ties to enrich himself. However, this hardly made him unique in the North Korean system. He did seem to accumulate enough power and influence with deep links to North Korea's main institutions to pose a theoretical risk to Kim Jong Un's leadership. Foreign observers speculated that Jang or his wife, Kim Kyong Hui, or both of them, might serve as a regent for the young Kim. Kim Kyong Hui was Kim Jong Un's aunt by blood, the daughter of the nation's founder. Jang Song Thaek had entered the top of the ruling class by marriage and was not part of the sacred Kim bloodline. Kim Jong Un dramatically demonstrated he was his own man and was not constrained by anyone, including Jang.

North Korea publicized Jang's arrest, conviction, and execution at home and abroad. Kim Jong Un messaged North Korean elites that he was in charge and no one—not even a powerful family member—was beyond his reach. Simultaneously, Kim demonstrated to the world that he was not a nominal leader of North Korea but the real power center.

Why did Kim Jong Un assassinate his half-brother?

In 2017, North Korean agents convinced two women to spray a substance in the face of a man at an airport in Kuala Lumpur, Malaysia. The women said they were duped into believing the act was a harmless prank for a TV show, but the substance was one of the most potent chemical weapons on earth, VX nerve agent. The target, apparently unbeknownst to the women, was Kim Jong Un's elder half-brother, Kim Jong Nam.

North Korean authorities denied involvement in the hit, but the public evidence was striking. The women implicated North Korean agents, saying they had provided them with the substance and identified the target. Kim Jong Un had a direct link to Kim Jong Nam and a rationale for eliminating him. More importantly, few nations have access to this VX nerve agent; North Korea is among them. The basic facts left little doubt that North Korea orchestrated the assassination. Given the importance of the target and fallout for the use of chemical weapons like this, it is difficult to conceive how the assassination could have gone forward without Kim Jong Un's direct order.

North Korean agents have many ways to kill. The decision to use an uncommon chemical weapon made it easier to trace the assassins back to the North Korean state. Pyongyang certainly would understand this simple point. The dramatic effort against a high-level target showed North Koreans everywhere that the regime would spare no expense to track down and brutally kill those deemed in any way threatening. Not even members of the Kim bloodline would be spared.

The Malaysian government was irate that North Korea would carry out an assassination and use chemical weapons in the airport of its capital city. Malaysia cut diplomatic relations with North Korea. The location of the hit appeared purposeful, not because of where the attack took place, but because where the attack did not take place. North Korea has no beef with Malaysia, but Kim Jong Un would not want to get cross with Beijing by trying to kill Kim Jong Nam in Chinese territory, where he lived. Unlike ties with China, the relationship with Malaysia was expendable.

Who is South Korean President Moon Jae-in?

South Korean president Moon Jae-in was elected in 2017, following his predecessor's impeachment and removal from office over an influence-peddling scandal. Simply remaining scandal-free would prove a major asset with which the new president could contrast himself with his wildly unpopular predecessor, Park Geun-hye, but Moon's signature policy effort beyond hosting the 2018 Winter Olympics would focus on North Korea.

President Moon's North Korea policy shares some elements of the policies of his progressive predecessors from a decade earlier, but he has more formally recognized that inter-Korean rapprochement must accompany US–North Korea negotiations in order to make progress on core security issues. North Korea defines the United States, not South Korea, as its main security threat. The North says it has developed nuclear weapons to deter US invasion, since it believes it can handle the South Korean military with its formidable conventional forces and thousands of artillery tubes aimed at Seoul. Consequently, Moon cannot address the nuclear issue and push forward inter-Korean cooperation in a meaningful and sustainable way without bringing the United States along.

When President Moon came to office in 2017, he offered to engage North Korea diplomatically, but North Korea was not yet ready to reciprocate. In 2017, US–North Korea rhetoric heated up with colorful threats. North Korea threatened to attack US bases in Japan, Hawaii, Alaska, and Guam. President Trump threatened "fire and fury" in response and engaged in name-calling with the North Korean leader. North Korea tested its intercontinental ballistic missile three times in 2017 to put the continental United States in range of its nuclear weapons as well. However, by the end of 2017, Kim Jong Un declared his nuclear deterrent complete and started 2018 with a different tack.

In early 2018, Kim Jong Un pursued inter-Korean dialogue on the discrete question of North Korea's participation in the fast-approaching Winter Olympics in South Korea. President Moon accepted, and the two Koreas fielded a pan-Korean team in limited sports. Moon offered the senior North Korean delegation visiting for the Olympics, including Kim Jong Un's trusted younger sister Kim Yo Jong, a prominent place with him—and the US vice president—in the viewing stand at the Olympics' opening ceremony.

Moon tried to play the role of peacemaker and extended the inter-Korean engagement beyond the Olympics. In April, Moon met Kim Jong Un at Panmunjom, which straddles the inter-Korean boundary in the middle of the DMZ. Moon was careful to consult closely with Washington and keep it on board with his vision. Kim Jong Un offered an unprecedented summit meeting with President Trump, who immediately accepted it. The US and North Korean leaders met in Singapore on June 12, 2018, sketching out the broad principles of a follow-on negotiation on denuclearization.

President Moon credited Trump for his leadership in meeting with Kim, but the whole episode was crafted carefully by Moon and his administration. Moon lavished praise on the American president, even publicly endorsing Trump's comment that he would welcome a Nobel Peace Prize for his efforts. Moon actively sought to avoid taking international credit for any success, something Trump did with apparent relish. President Moon came to power only in 2017, but his North Korea initiative is already shaping up to be the signature effort of his presidency. It remains to be seen if the gambit will be successful, but Moon has shown a willingness to take a political gamble on North Korea engagement while successfully managing the relationship with the United States.

8

INTER-KOREAN RELATIONS IN THE TWENTY-FIRST CENTURY

What were the inter-Korean summits?

North Korean leaders have agreed to meet with all three of South Korea's progressive presidents but have refused to meet any of its conservative ones. South Korean conservatives toe a harder line on North Korea, including on security issues and human rights, so they have had a more difficult time encouraging North Korea to engage on this topic. South Korean conservatives often want to include the nuclear issue as a substantive part of the inter-Korean agenda, for example, while North Korea insists on discussing the specifics of nuclear issue with the United States. South Korean progressives, by contrast, focus inter-Korean meetings more on discreet economic and cultural cooperation projects and hope improved relations will assist security discussions in other venues.

In the first inter-Korean summit, in 2000, South Korean president Kim Dae-jung met North Korean leader Kim Jong Il. The summit initiated or advanced a series of economic projects and cultural exchanges. Inter-Korean economic projects like the Kaesong Industrial Complex (KIC) and the Mount Kumgang tourist site took years to develop across multiple South Korean presidential administrations and had some longevity beyond Kim Dae-jung's term. However, the summit came under greater criticism after it was revealed years later that Kim Dae-jung had orchestrated a $500 million payment to North Korea to secure the meeting.

The second inter-Korean summit in 2007 had less lasting effect. South Korean president Roh Moo-hyun sought the meeting even as his own five-year term was coming to a close. Two months before a South Korean presidential election would tap a conservative with a decidedly different view of North Korea policy to lead the country, Roh penned an ambitious liberal agenda with Kim Jong Il. The summit agreement included a joint fishing zone in waters replete with North-South naval clashes, expanded economic cooperation and pledges of aid, and reaffirmed previous North Korean nuclear commitments. However, the two sides never implemented the 2007 summit agreement; the incoming South Korean president, Lee Myung-bak, had no intention of being bound by his lame duck predecessor's eleventh-hour executive agreement.

In 2018, South Korean president Moon Jae-in held the third inter-Korean summit with Kim Jong Un. Unlike the prior two summits, this one was not held in North Korea's capital. Instead, the two leaders met in Panmunjom on the inter-Korean boundary in the middle of the DMZ. Unscripted, Kim invited Moon to step into North Korean territory, and Moon reciprocated. The otherwise carefully choreographed event was heavy on symbolism. Moon's government closely coordinated with Washington and played broker to help set up the first US–North Korea summit less than two months later to chart a path forward on denuclearization. Moon and Kim met again in May 2018, on less than forty-eight-hours' notice. The follow-on summit lacked the earlier meeting's pomp and circumstance but demonstrated the two leaders were willing and able to engage on pressing policy issues on short notice. In September 2018, Moon traveled to Pyongyang for yet another summit as inter-Korean contact at the top reached new highs.

What were the North-South joint economic ventures at Kaesong and Mt. Kumgang?

North-South joint ventures intended to improve political relations, introduce South Korean business practices in limited ways to North Koreans, and even pave the way for a long-term unification of the two Koreas. The two most important projects were the Kaesong Industrial Complex (KIC) and the Mount Kumgang Tourist Resort.

The KIC, situated in the historic city of Kaesong just north of the DMZ, housed a variety of simple South Korean manufacturing businesses. South Korea provided the managers and capital, and North Korea provided the labor. The enterprises sought to turn a profit off the low cost of North Korean labor but could only survive with insurance provided by the South Korean government. The risk that either Korean government could shut down the entire project if relations soured again was simply too great to make the project genuinely commercially viable. However, the South Korean government was willing to guarantee the South Korean companies' investments in order to attempt the reconciliation experiment. The two Koreas constantly negotiated terms of access to the complex, but the KIC closed in 2016 after inter-Korean relations again turned downward.

The Mount Kumgang Tourist Resort on North Korea's east coast was the other most important inter-Korean economic project. An affiliate of the Hyundai group, Hyundai-Asan, invested in the scenic resort with permission of the two governments. When it opened, South Korean tourists curious to get a glimpse of North Korea were ferried up the east coast of the peninsula to the coastal tourist site.

When, in 2008, a middle-aged female South Korean tourist went walking along the beach before dawn one morning and passed a military exclusion zone, a North Korean guard shot her dead. The incident caused an outcry in South Korea, and Seoul demanded an investigation and apology. North Korea refused, calling the shooting a "self-defense measure."[1] The conservative South Korean government, long wary of the project that had been begun under its progressive predecessors, prohibited South Korean nationals from visiting the tourist zone. North Korea attempted to market the resort to other groups, primarily to Chinese tourists, but it never took off as it had when South Koreans visited. The inter-Korean project was dead.

A progressive president leads South Korea again today, but there is not the same focus on these enclaves as during the Sunshine era. President Moon seems to recognize the Trump administration's concern about moves that may undercut economic sanctions and has prioritized noneconomic areas for inter-Korean cooperation for the time being. The time for inter-Korean economic projects is not done, but it is suspended at least for now.

What are inter-Korean family reunions?

Family reunions are an effort to allow close family members separated by the division of the Korean nation to meet for short events. These reunions are negotiated and planned either by governmental organs directly or by semigovernmental organizations such as the two sides' Red Cross representatives. Family reunions are widely popular in South Korea on humanitarian grounds, and both conservative and progressive administrations have pursued them. Gauging the public opinion is more difficult in North Korea, but they are presumably supported there for similar reasons. The reunions allow elderly Koreans to see their close relatives one last time before they die.

Family reunions require governmental involvement, because both Koreas legally prohibit their nationals from traveling to the other state. Legacy laws from the Cold War period preclude South Koreans from traveling to or telephoning anyone in North Korea. Commercial phone lines do not connect the two countries, and North Koreans lack free access to the Internet to make use of more modern forms of communication. North Koreans are likewise banned from visiting South Korea, and even permanent defectors looking to resettle in South Korea face long prison terms if they are caught trying to make it to South Korea. Unable to visit family through private travel, long-separated family members must get the two governments to agree to set up the emotionally charged meetings if they are to meet again.

What is the North Korean artillery threat to Seoul?

North Korea maintains approximately eight thousand artillery tubes forward deployed along the DMZ, and a portion of them are able to range metropolitan Seoul. North Korea could inflict enormous damage on the northern suburbs of Seoul if it chooses to unleash this terror threat. North Korea also maintains a more modest array of long-range artillery, which is more likely intended for military targets.[2]

The North Korean artillery threat to Seoul is tremendously significant but also often overstated. North Korea cannot level the sprawling South Korean capital. Most of its artillery cannot even reach downtown Seoul. However, the regime could impose very high civilian casualties in the opening days and hours of a war. Threatening to impose unacceptable consequences is the purpose of deterrence. The North Korean artillery does this for the South Korean government. For a variety of reasons, including the North Korean artillery threat, it is inconceivable that the South Korean military would attempt a preemptive strike on North Korea.[3]

Nevertheless, the presence of the North Korean artillery creates an aura that Seoul lives under the constant possibility of a North Korean barrage. In 2010, North Korea carried out two major provocations. In March, it sank a South Korean naval vessel, the *Cheonan*, killing forty-six sailors. In November, it shelled a remote South Korean island off the North Korean coast with artillery fire, killing four. Both events were tragic, but South Koreans reacted much more to the artillery strike, which had less than one-tenth the number of casualties. The shelling was a reminder that North Korea had much more robust artillery capabilities aimed at their social, political, and economic capital in Seoul.

What was the Cheonan sinking?

In 2010, the South Korean naval corvette called the *Cheonan* sank off South Korea's west coast in what Koreans call the West Sea and most international maps refer to as the Yellow Sea. The shallow and muddy body of water is ripe for submarines, and North Korea operates a fleet of submarines in this space. An international investigation concluded that a North Korean torpedo sank the South Korean vessel, killing forty-six South Korean sailors onboard.[4] North Korea denied any involvement, and some international observers cast doubt on the investigation without presenting a verifiable alternative explanation for the ship's sinking.[5]

South Korea responded by cutting off all trade with North Korea except the KIC. (The complex would later close for separate reasons.) South Korea also instituted new rules of military engagement that promised far greater retaliation for any North Korean attack. US military officials worried that the new rules of engagement risked unwanted conflict escalation that could get out of control. It stimulated a long negotiation within the US–South Korean alliance on the proper response to these types of North Korean actions. The allies called the resulting agreement the Counter Provocation Plan.

Within months of the *Cheonan* sinking, North Korea shelled a South Korean island called Yeonpyeong-do. The source of this attack was unmistakable and quieted the remaining debate over North Korean culpability in the *Cheonan* sinking. Under either interpretation of the cause of the *Cheonan* sinking—a North Korean torpedo or something else—Seoul could justify its strong response based on North Korea's follow-up violence in the artillery strike.

What was the Yeonpyeong-do shelling?

In November 2010, just months after the sinking of the *Cheonan*, North Korea shelled a South Korean island called Yeonpyeong-do. The island is located just off the North Korean coast in South Korea's northwest islands. South Korean civilians and marines live on the island, and the North Korean shelling killed two South Korean civilians and two marines. North Korea said the attack was a response to South Korea's live fire exercise that shot into North Korean territorial waters, which landed in the sea.[6]

The West Sea is a common flashpoint for inter-Korean skirmishes. Since the two sides disagree on the maritime boundary between them, both argue that the other side's fishing or coast guard vessels are crossing illegally into their waters. North Korea argues that the maritime boundary between the two Koreas should extend directly from the land boundary. Since this boundary slopes southward as it nears the West Sea, North Korea prefers a line that cuts diagonally to the south to expand its own waters. South Korea prefers the Northern Limit Line (NLL), which hugs the North Korean west coast and proceeds northward around the northwest islands of South Korean territory and includes Yeonpyeong-do. The NLL was a line that the Americans drew in the 1950s to limit how far north they would permit South Korean forces to venture as the United States sought to constrain South Korea from escalating conflict or seeking unification in a way that could embroil Washington in an even longer and bloodier war. South Korea interprets the NLL as the boundary between the two Koreas.

The Yeonpyeong-do shelling inflamed South Korean public opinion. It marked the first time since the Korean War that

North Korea had shelled South Korean territory with artillery. It stood as a stark reminder that North Korea posed a much bigger artillery threat to Seoul as well.

Why did the North-South joint ventures at Kaesong and Mt. Kumgang end?

The North-South economic projects hoped to use economic cooperation to facilitate economic, political, and social reconciliation between the two Koreas, which had grown far apart over decades of division and divergent governance models. The projects withstood multiple North Korean provocations, including lethal attacks and testing associated with the country's development of nuclear-tipped missiles. With the South Korean public's patience with the peace experiment growing thin, new North Korean actions against South Korean interests shut down the economic projects one by one.

In 2008, after the inauguration of the first conservative South Korean president after the ten years of progressive rule that set the economic projects in place, a North Korean guard shot and killed a South Korean tourist who ventured into a prohibited zone just after dawn, down the beach from the Mount Kumgang Resort. South Korea called for an investigation into the shooting incident, which some conservative commentators were starting to call a "murder," and demanded an apology. North Korean state media called the event a self-defense measure, and the regime refused to take part in a joint investigation. The Lee Myung-bak government was no fan of the economic project, but North Korea's behavior made deciding how to react easier. Citing concern for the safety of South Korean citizens, Seoul prohibited its people from visiting the resort on the North Korean east coast. North Korea attempted unsuccessfully to market the resort to other countries' citizens, especially Chinese tourists. The Mount Kumgang Resort would continue to operate for special events such as the occasional inter-Korean family reunion, but the inter-Korean economic project was effectively over.

Nevertheless, South Korea localized its response to the shooting to the Mount Kumgang project, preventing it from affecting other inter-Korean projects. South Korean business managers and government officials continued to travel to the KIC, just north of the DMZ, in particular, to keep the project moving. When North Korea torpedoed a South Korean naval vessel, the *Cheonan*, in 2010, killing forty-six sailors, the Blue House called for an international investigation even as its defense ministry wanted to strike back. The international investigation into what caused the sudden sinking of the ship dragged on for months and finally determined that a North Korean torpedo was the only reasonable conclusion. South Korea responded with more robust rules of engagement, which gave its military commanders more latitude to respond with greater force. South Korean military leaders seemed to understand they had political support from the South Korean president to retaliate aggressively and immediately.

Seoul also instituted new sanctions—the 5.24 measures, as they are known in South Korea, denoting the date of enactment of May 24. The May 24 measures ended all inter-Korean economic contact except through the KIC. The KIC had accounted for the majority of inter-Korean trade before the measures but became the last vestige of inter-Korean cooperation after the new sanction.

Years later, the KIC, too, would close. Another conservative South Korean administration had tolerated the legacy inter-Korean project, but it would not survive North Korea's further testing of its nuclear and missile forces. After the fourth North Korean nuclear test, in January 2016—but the first under the Park Geun-hye administration, which repeatedly attempted to cast number four as a "game-changer"—Seoul looked to retaliate diplomatically. The following month, North Korea poked again, launching another long-range rocket. The Park administration responded by pulling the plug on the KIC. Both sides pointed fingers and blamed the other for the industrial park's closure.

The Sunshine era's tools of engagement were now all out of use. When a new South Korean progressive returned to the Blue House in 2017, he would seek to chart his own new path toward inter-Korean reconciliation.

9

THE ECONOMY

Is North Korea economically self-reliant?

North Korean leader Kim Il Sung first declared his emphasis on self-reliance in a 1955 speech. Encapsulating self-reliance of all forms in the *Juche* ideology, North Korea, too, envisioned an economic model that did not give undue influence to any single foreign power. However, North Korea simply lacked the national wherewithal to be a truly self-reliant country. Indeed, Kim Il Sung built a North Korean foreign affairs strategy that oscillated between Soviet and Chinese benefactors to avoid giving either too much influence over him.

Ironically, North Korea has grown more economically self-reliant, or autarkic, as it has become weaker and more isolated internationally. North Korean heavy industry relied on foreign supplied energy during the Cold War, but the severe energy crunch that North Korea faced after the Soviet collapse shrank the North Korean heavy industrial sector. North Korean agriculture's reliance on petroleum-based fertilizers with foreign inputs likewise shrank in the 1990s as the regime experimented with new methods to incentivize domestic agricultural output. North Korea's efforts to cope with increased international isolation and lessened foreign support has made it more self-sufficient.

China makes up about 90 percent of North Korean trade today. Kim Il Sung, who sought to limit dependence on any one foreign backer by exploiting differences between Moscow and Beijing in the Sino-Soviet split, must be turning over in his mausoleum. China's tremendous share of North Korean trade has less to do with expanding Chinese penetration of the North Korean market and more to do with North Korea's loss of other trade partners. However, North Korea is not a trading state at its core; its total trade (imports plus exports) amount to about 12.5 percent of its GDP. By contrast, South Korea is a trading state and its total trade stands at 110 percent of GDP.[1]

North Korea traded with socialist and non-aligned states during the Cold War. This shrank after the Cold War ended. By the early 2000s, the vast majority of North Korea's trade volume was captured by a small number of its neighbors. China was its biggest import and export partner, but Japan was the second-largest export market for North Korea until 2006. After North Korea resumed long-range missile flight tests in 2006, Tokyo cut it off. Japanese consumers would find their fishery products elsewhere, but North Korea lost a key export market. A few years later, in 2010, South Korea, North Korea's largest trading partner after China at the time, also cut off all trade except for the Kaesong Industrial Complex. The Kaesong Industrial Complex closed too in 2016 following another series of North Korean nuclear and missile provocations. North Korea self-isolated and created a situation where China dominated both its import and export opportunities.

North Korea uses autarky to limit foreign influence. It grows most of its own food, which insulates itself from the political risks of trade pressure. The self-reliance mantra limits economic opportunities and efficiency afforded by comparative-advantage trade. As such, the marginal cost to North Korea from additional foreign sanctions is low, but the potential marginal benefits of easing sanctions could be high. Imposing new sanctions on North Korea and offering sanctions relief are two sides of the same coin. However, there is greater room for movement on sanctions relief than there are creative efforts to find new ways to further squeeze a regime economically that is already cut off from most of the world economically.

Who are North Korea's major trading partners?

China accounts for roughly 90 percent of North Korean trade today. The remainder is a potpourri of smaller business partners. North Korea sought throughout its history to diversify its trade (and aid) partners to limit its political dependence on any one state. It managed this delicate dance decently well to advance the political objective of "self-reliance" during the Cold War, but it failed in this objective in the post–Cold War era.

North Korea owed its earliest forms of external support to the Soviet Union. After the victors in World War II, including the United States and the Soviet Union, divided the Korean Peninsula in 1945, the two emerging superpowers supported Korean governments they hoped would be friendly to them and locally sustainable. Within five years, Kim Il Sung started the Korean War after discussion primarily with Soviet leader Joseph Stalin, but also Chinese leader Mao Zedong. Within months, China intervened militarily to thwart Kim's military defeat, suffering hundreds of thousands of casualties to the US–South Korea force. North Korea depended on various types of support from Moscow and Beijing, including preferential trade, aid, and even military and political support. As the Cold War progressed and Moscow and Beijing feuded, North Korea played the two off of each other. In this way, North Korea tried to avoid economic dependence on either state.

After the collapse of the Soviet Union in 1990, North Korea refused to honor its Soviet-era debt to the successor Russian government. With Moscow's appetite for supporting Pyongyang already diminished, North Korea–Russia trade plummeted in 1991. China became North Korea's largest trading partner by default but gradually took on more trade and aid roles with North Korea. South Korea rose to become

North Korea's second-largest trading partner as a result of Sunshine era economic projects, but this would reverse itself dramatically when inter-Korean trade returned to near zero a few years later. North Korea also alienated Japan with its nuclear tests, and Tokyo went from importing more from North Korea than any other state except China to banning all North Korean imports. During the Cold War, North Korea had a reasonably diversified set of trade partners for a country in its position, but its increasing international isolation in the last quarter century made it more dependent on a single foreign partner, China.

Since North Korea does not publish official trade data as most countries do, economists are left to construct "mirror statistics." The amount of goods that Japan, for example, imports from North Korea is the same as the amount that North Korea exports to Japan. North Korea does not publish the amount of its exports to Japan, but we can use the Japanese numbers to fill in this data point. Doing this for all North Korea's trade partners allows one to construct a balance sheet of North Korean trade.

North Korea also does not publish the amount of development and humanitarian aid that it receives, leaving one to use a similar method to estimate North Korea's aid levels. International organizations like the UN and major nongovernmental organizations (NGOs) also provide aid to North Korea, so constructing an estimate of North Korea's aid must go beyond the national government data that was used to estimate its trade. Adding together international organization, NGO, and national aid begins to paint a picture of North Korea's aid receipts.

Unfortunately, North Korea's trade and aid data constructed through mirror statistics is not as complete as it could be. China does not publish its level of aid to North Korea, which is likely significant, and even the reliability of its data on China–North Korea trade can be questionable. North Korea also trades "off the books." For example, Iran does not include ballistic missile imports from North Korea in its official trade data. Syria did not have a line item for the nuclear weapons assistance purchased from North Korea either. When North Korea trafficked opium, sold counterfeit cigarettes, or smuggled products such as endangered species through its embassies, abusing its diplomatic privilege to avoid customs, none of these illicit activities factored into the mirror statistics.

Researchers can and have estimated North Korean trade and aid, but it requires some tolerance for ambiguity. Some have even attempted to include the illicit trade in their estimates to capture a broader view of North Korea's foreign trade. Even precise numbers underlie considerable uncertainty in the data, and readers should look at these figures as general estimates.[2]

Who are South Korea's major trading partners?

China is South Korea's largest trading partner by far today. Bilateral South Korea–China trade accounts for over $211 billion in total trade, representing about a quarter of South Korea's trade with the world. South Korea's trade with its second largest trading partner, the United States, accounts for just over half the China total. US–South Korea total trade amounted to $110 billion, or 12 percent of South Korea's trade with the world. South Korea retains a comprehensive import and export relationship with Japan and has a diversified array of trade partners in other areas.[3] For example, the energy-starved nation imports considerable oil and gas from Middle East suppliers and has looked to export nuclear power plants to the same countries, most notably agreeing to build nuclear power plants in the United Arab Emirates.[4] It exports intermediate goods to Mexico that are ultimately destined for the American market. South Korea also trades with its regional neighbors, most significantly Hong Kong, Australia, the Philippines, Singapore, and Taiwan.[5]

While the composition of South Korea's trade is important in its own right, the more significant story is the dramatic change in its trade patterns. Near the end of the Cold War, in 1988, Japan supplied over 30 percent of South Korea's imports and the United States about 25 percent. South Korea's trade with China was negligible, amounting to a small fraction of South Korea's total imports, and diverted through Hong Kong to mainland China. However, China's general economic expansion made it a supplier of goods to many countries in the world, including South Korea. By 2016, China accounted for over 20 percent of all South Korean imports, and the United States and Japan dropped to just over 10 percent each. South Korea's export destinations tell much the same story of the rapid increase of China trade amid the relative decline of the US and Japanese markets.

What these data do not show is South Korea's diversified imports and exports with a number of countries throughout the globe. Most of South Korea's trade partners amount to less than 5 percent of its imports or exports, but this miscellaneous

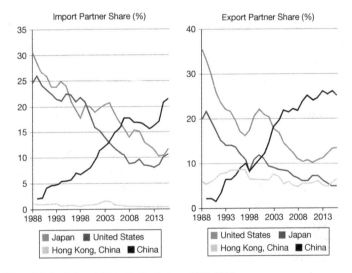

Figure 9.1 South Korea's Major Trading Partners, 1998–2014

Source: World Bank

group of trading partners as a whole accounts for more of South Korea's trade than the top three put together. South Korea is an advanced trading state, selling its goods and services in every corner of the globe and buying there too.

What sanctions are imposed on North Korea?

North Korea faces a web of multilateral sanctions authorized by the UN Security Council and unilateral sanctions imposed by individual national governments. For example, the United States has blocked virtually all North Korean trade with US companies and institutions. It has encouraged other states to do the same, since US sanctions policy has developed increasingly sophisticated tools to try to further isolate North Korea from international markets.

The UN Security Council has passed a series of resolutions condemning North Korean actions related to its nuclear and ballistic missile development. The council has called North Korea's nuclear and missile programs a threat to international peace and stability. It imposed multilateral sanctions that require all UN member states, which is basically the entire world, to enforce the sanctions. The sanctions focused initially on blocking North Korean access to inputs for its nuclear and missile programs and were relatively noncontroversial. A German company, for example, could not sell components of rocket engines to North Korea. German authorities would be responsible for policing this activity within their jurisdiction and reporting findings to the UN. Later multilateral sanctions would bar legal trade in a variety of areas, most notably North Korean coal exports, to impose more general and less targeted economic pain on the country.

North Korea's nuclear tests and missile launches continued, and the UN sanctions grew more robust on paper and in reality. The UN barred states from selling North Korea "luxury goods," which led some fancy companies to claim their goods were not luxurious. The UN sought to plug such holes by creating lists of luxury goods and encouraging member states to broadly enforce the sanctions. The UN Panel of Experts that focuses on this specific set of UN sanctions on North Korea repeatedly determined the biggest challenge to sanctions effectiveness was enforcement.[6] Most countries in the world do not have the government capacity or will to cull UN lists and closely monitor their companies' imports and exports to North Korea. Small African or Asian countries may determine they have more pressing priorities, for example.

Nevertheless, the UN Security Council sanctions are significant, because North Korea's most important trade partner and patron, China, has a permanent seat on the council. Security Council deliberations on North Korea sanctions, in practice, often devolve into a US-China or US-China-Russia discussion. The United Kingdom and France, the other two countries that round out the veto-wielding permanent council members, generally support the US advocacy on this matter, and only the veto-wielding permanent five members on the council are most intimately engaged in the negotiations. Consequently, Security Council sanctions are in large part a venue to urge China to impose more economic pressure on North Korea.

Beyond the UN sanctions, individual countries can prohibit their companies from trading with or investing in North Korea for a variety of reasons. American law has a long series of overlapping sanctions on North Korea. The United States sanctions North Korea because of its nuclear program, missile development, weapons of mass destruction proliferation, human rights abuses, drug trafficking, counterfeiting of US products and currency, state support for terrorism, money laundering, its status as a communist and socialist state, and other reasons. The North Koreans have noted publicly that they understand lifting particular sanctions will have no direct economic effect, because other overlapping sanctions will still block the same trade.[7]

Other countries have their own restrictions on trade with North Korea beyond Security Council mandates. South Korea and Japan have widespread bans on trade with North Korea. The United States and its allies also actively encourage smaller states to block specific transactions that may violate UN sanctions or otherwise present a threat to the country's national interest. When encouragement is insufficient in sanctions diplomacy, Washington also relies on more powerful tools to isolate North Korea economically.

"Secondary sanctions" are a US tool that targets foreign companies outside American jurisdiction to dissuade them from doing business with North Korea. These sanctions effectively make foreign companies choose between trading with the United States and American companies and using the US financial system, on the one hand, or pursuing business with North Korea, on the other. Few international companies in today's interconnected marketplace choose to do business with North Korea instead of the United States.

What would sanctions relief mean for North Korea?

North Korea values sanctions relief, even if it is primarily symbolic. In particular, the United States' loosening its unilateral sanctions on North Korea sends an important signal to the rest of the world. Whether defensible or not on the technical merits of the regulations, other states see the United States' removing North Korea from one sanctions list in more general terms. Any sanctions relief sends the message that Washington is loosening, not tightening, economic pressure on North Korea. Other states may relax their own enforcement of unrelated UN restrictions on North Korean trade as a result. Just as the effectiveness of new sanction authorities must be judged by their enforced value in further squeezing North Korea, sanctions relief must be understood for the effective impact of the policy shift rather than for the implications on paper alone.

However, even comprehensive sanctions relief is unlikely to stimulate substantial new trade and investment in North Korea. Surveys of Chinese traders document the abysmal trade infrastructure in North Korea. The country's roads, rail, and ports are dilapidated. Its cell-phone network is not connected to the rest of the world. Corruption is rampant, requiring bribes and delays. And North Korean law does not respect contracts or property rights. Add to this the reputational risk of doing business with the world's worst human rights violator, ever-present chance of the reimposition of sanctions, and lack of North Korean products of high international value, and it is difficult to make a business case for investing or trading with North Korea even if sanctions are completely removed.

The Iran nuclear deal exposed some of these problems. Although Iran did have something of high international value—namely, oil—and the trade challenges it posed were far less than those posed by North Korea, Iran was still disappointed that the sanctions relief from a 2015 nuclear deal did not produce the kind of economic growth it hoped and expected. Neither the imposition of new sanctions nor sanctions relief alone is likely to have a major impact on North Korean decision-making on core security issues like the nuclear program.

What are North Korea's special economic zones?

Special economic zones (SEZs) are small enclaves where the rules of business are different than the rest of the country. In heavily regulated markets like North Korea's, SEZs promise some relief from that strong governmental presence and a more permissive business environment. The small zones also allow a national government like North Korea to test different approaches to economic management.

North Korea first experimented with SEZs in 1992 with the opening of the Rajin-Sonbong, or Rason, Special Economic Zone in the northeast corner of the country. It was important news at the time that North Korea might be experimenting with alternative economic models, but the zone did not produce new national economic policy.

Other SEZs include the Kaesong Industrial Complex and the Mount Kumgang tourist site. Both of these SEZs sought to attract South Korean business to North Korea and improve inter-Korean relations, but both have been subsequently shuttered after political disputes. Another SEZ just south of the China–North Korean border at Sinuiju likewise hoped to gain more Chinese investors interested in North Korea. Indeed, in 2013, Kim Jong Un started to roll out over a dozen new SEZs with little impact on the broader national economy.[8]

10

KOREAN SOCIETY

NORTH AND SOUTH

What is North Korea's Songbun social classification system?

After the Korean War, North Korea's founder and leader Kim Il Sung aggressively moved to enhance his personal power at the top of the North Korean system. He continued to purge individuals and factions that he judged less than completely loyal to him. North Korea's most significant foreign patrons, most notably the Soviets, watched and worried as Kim built a cult of personality around himself. As his effort to purge potential rivals among the political class progressed, Kim turned to a more comprehensive effort to ensure personal loyalty at every level of society.

Kim Il Sung's North Korea had long imposed punishments without reference to rule of law against those it deemed a threat. However, Pyongyang went beyond trying to prosecute political crimes to preempting them. In the 1960s, Kim Il Sung ordered a comprehensive investigation of members of society to classify them according to political loyalty. Family background was critical, and the stakes for individuals could hardly have been higher.

Kim Il Sung was crafty enough not to simply create a small elite lavished with privilege against the rest of society. He constructed a social system, which was called the Songbun system, with gradations of benefits. Beyond the "core" class at the very top, the regime classified families into a middle "wavering" class and a bottom "hostile" class. There is a more detailed mechanism for classifying individuals as well, but this more general overlay explains the broad brushstrokes of the North Korean social system. A hierarchical social order based on one's family background was nothing new in Korea, but Songbun was unique in doling out privilege to families based on their loyalty to the Kim regime.

Those families classified as most loyal, especially the three hundred fighters who fought alongside Kim Il Sung during the guerrilla campaign against Japanese colonialism, won the most prized positions in society. They and their descendants would occupy the senior positions of the Korean Workers' Party and Korean People's Army. They would enjoy higher wages, social prestige, better educational and occupational opportunities for their children, access to state-run vacation spots, and better medical care. In short, they enjoyed the best material and intangible benefits that the regime could confer.

Kim Il Sung built a loyal elite. Those in positions of power would not only take incredible risks for themselves by opposing the Kim regime, but they knew their families would be severely punished as well for their disloyalty. Kim Il Sung relied on ideological indoctrination and repression to maintain control, but the material and intangible benefits afforded to those at the top of the Songbun system were among the most important tools of regime maintenance.

Those in the middle "wavering" class had little opportunity to move up. They could earn entrance into a second-tier college, for example, and earn a living as a government technocrat or provincial white-collar worker, but they could not aspire to higher positions based on personal merit without the right Songbun. This would be perennially disappointing for any ambitious individual, but the implicit threat of falling into the "hostile" class would prove an important motivator for those in the middle to not cross the regime.

Those at the bottom faced the greatest hardships in North Korea. Their perceived potential disloyalty to the leader ensured they would be excluded from power. They would be denied the tools of human capital development, such as higher education. They would be kept away from the capital city of Pyongyang and kept busy working in the most difficult jobs in agriculture and industry. Those deemed particularly hostile, such as the family members of defectors, collaborators with the Japanese colonialists, and "factionalists" deemed disloyal to the Kim family, would find themselves assigned to hard manual labor such as coal mining, put in prison, or worse.

North Korea's social system serves the leader, not the country or the people. It is part of an Orwellian effort to comprehensively control threats and preempt them. It is tremendously discriminatory and contrary to ideal notions of social mobilization based on individual merit. Other societies certainly face challenges to pure meritocracy and social privilege based on such factors as family wealth, but the North Korea system is distinct as a governmentally directed and maintained systematic effort to assign social benefits to serve the exclusive interest of the North Korean leader.[1]

What does it mean to be a North Korean elite?

The North Korean elite are the top class in North Korean society who gain privilege based on their family background and assumption of loyalty to the leader. They are overwhelmingly concentrated in the North Korean capital of Pyongyang, enjoy prestigious jobs, and attend the country's top educational institutions. They enjoy the most comfortable state-provided housing, more balanced diets, access to recreational facilities and better medical care, and even prospects of foreign travel and gifts of luxury goods from the leader.

Living in Pyongyang is considered a privilege in North Korea, and the state determines who can live, or even visit, the capital. The city houses the country's most significant monuments and public squares. The city hosts the country's largest parades, festivals, and cultural and entertainment opportunities. Those living outside Pyongyang are inculcated with the belief that it is a special opportunity and reward just to get to visit the city. Living in Pyongyang has concrete advantages over the countryside, but it is also prestigious. The intangibles of prestige can be powerful motivating factors in human behavior, and the North Korean regime actively seeks to define and supply prestige to serve its purpose of controlling society.

North Korea's most prestigious institutions—places of work and study—are also in Pyongyang. Jobs in the Korean Workers' Party and the upper echelons of the Korean People's Army top the social ladder. These individuals have the chance to participate in some small way in national decisions and most directly serve the leader. They also earn the highest wages. They come from a select group of institutions of higher learning, not because Kim Il Sung University trains even its bottom student better than the top graduate of provincial schools, but because it is a step in the chain of supporting the most loyal families. North Korean elites know they are guaranteed a certain level of social success as long as they do not cross the Kim family.

North Korean elites enjoy some basic benefits of daily living over the masses. The state allocates housing, so the elite naturally get the homes considered most valuable. In capitalist societies, those who can pay gain access to housing that is deemed most valuable according to price. In North Korea, political loyalty rather than money determines this access. The state also has traditionally allocated food. North Koreans today lack a healthy diet. As a society, they have insufficient amounts of meat and protein in their diet. Malnutrition rates are high compared to North Korea's Northeast Asian neighbors. The elite are not free from the country's food-insecurity problem, but they are much less likely to go hungry or feed their children an unbalanced diet that produces long-term health problems.

They eat more rice, which is prized in Korean society, as well as meat and luxury foods.

The regime also builds and runs recreational facilities and hospitals. It determines who is allowed to travel abroad legally. The elite can take advantage of a state-run ski resort, water parks, and festivals. When they get sick, the country's most well-stocked hospitals are at their disposal. If they need to travel outside North Korea, then they can get exit permission to legally depart and return home.

Lastly, the Kim regime also provides gifts in the form of luxury goods to those at the top. One may get a Rolex watch, fine cognac, foreign cigarettes, or even a Mercedes-Benz. These rewards are reserved for those at the very top and consequently have been a prime target of international sanctions, efforts to punish the regime rather than the disadvantaged members of North Korean society. Luxury goods may be the cherry on top of the icing on the cake, but their significance as a motivating factor or determinant of regime-provided privilege is often overstated. North Korea's ability to define a broad range of far more significant material and intangible incentives further encourages elite loyalty. In addition to the prospect of punishment or death in a successor regime, this creates a stunning contrast for North Korean elites and an effective structure to maintain elite loyalty.

The rise of markets and role of money in the last two decades has moderated this somewhat. Those who trade in the market can earn a better living than many workers in state enterprises. Especially when the regime failed to provide rations to its workers during the famine, this alternative employment on the fringes of legality provided desperate people a path to survival. It affected the country's social structure, especially among the middle and lower strata. However, a survey of defectors showed that they overwhelmingly still see the route to success in North Korea as running through party membership.[2] Marketization is an important phenomenon for those who cannot aspire to the top ranks of society, but it has not redefined the top that remains firmly state determined.

What is the status of women in North Korea?

North Korea claims to promote gender equality, and there's a grain of truth in its claim. On a variety of metrics of women's empowerment, including women's employment rates and wages, ability to serve in the military, educational attainment, and levels of health, North Korean women and girls fare similarly to their male counterparts.

At the top, North Korea's Politburo has had two female members but remains male-dominated. Kim Jong Un's aunt, Kim Kyong Hui, and his trusted younger sister, Kim Yo Jong, have occupied posts in the regime's highest political body. The Kim family bloodline is more important than gender in North Korea. But all three of North Korea's supreme leaders have been men, and there is no solid evidence a woman has ever been considered seriously for the job. North Korea watchers debate whether Kim Yo Jong, for example, could succeed her older brother if he suddenly died considering that his children are not yet ready for kindergarten let alone to run the country. The two sides are replete with guesses, but no one can know for sure because North Korea has never faced a succession without a designated male heir. The North Korean constitution provides no guide to this extraconstitutional familial succession.

Beyond the commanding heights of politics, North Korean women have more opportunity than do women in many countries at North Korea's level of development. North Korean girls go to school and the doctor, get fed as much as boys, and have many of the same basic advantages and hardships as their male counterparts. All young men are required to serve in the North Korean military, but the military does not exclude women. Photographs of top military brass are seas of men, but the lower levels provide some means for women to advance their standing through the military.

North Korean women are also employed at high rates. Even young mothers are encouraged and required to return to the workplace shortly after giving birth. The regime provides a short maternity leave but operates an extensive array of childcare centers. This allows the state to instill loyalty to the regime, rather than the family, from a very young age. Beyond their workplace responsibilities, men and women are required to participate in regime ideological study sessions, which further limits family time and more traditional connections between mothers and children. One can certainly dispute whether this is genuinely empowering to women, but it does raise North Korea's scores on cross-national metrics on the subject.

Perhaps more tellingly, North Korean women dominate the markets. They operate as retail traders and earn money even when their husband's state-provided job does not provide for the family as the real value of compensation in state industries has declined. North Korean women's role as primary breadwinners in these families has upended traditional family life. There have been anecdotal reports of increased domestic violence by men who resent their wives' newfound economic power even if it is keeping the family alive.

The regime has contributed to women's domination of the market sector by allowing only women over the age of fifty to trade legally. This attempts to restrict absenteeism by able-bodied men working in state industries who may otherwise be tempted by higher economic opportunity in markets. Ironically, the state's valuing women's labor less in state enterprises has given North Korean women more freedom to work in markets, where they can earn a higher income. The older women are also considered a lesser political threat to the regime. Middle-aged women are considered less likely than young men to organize as a potential fighting force that could challenge the regime if their power as a group grew considerably.

How does the North Korean government control society?

Pyongyang uses a series of carrots and sticks to encourage compliance with regime demands and prosecute perceived disloyalty. The Songbun social classification system, affording benefits to the elite, creates a strong incentive to maintain loyalty, a desire to keep those rewards for themselves and their families.

Ideology and information control are other regime tools to try to convince North Koreans to follow the Kim family rule. Pyongyang severely curtails access to outside information. North Korean TV and radio broadcasts exclusively promote regime messages. Listening to foreign broadcasts, such the Voice of America, Radio Free Asia, or a host of smaller radio stations by modifying official radios or using a smuggled radio is illegal. Watching South Korean dramas that have been smuggled across the China–North Korea border is also illegal but has grown more popular. Indeed, South Korean dramas have grown sufficiently popular that the regime has responded not only by punishing those caught watching the shows but also by improving the entertainment value of its own TV programs to keep its citizens from exposing themselves to nonregime ideas.

Beyond mass media, Pyongyang spreads regime ideology extensively. Beginning with state-run nurseries and continuing through higher education, North Korea teaches a political philosophy that serves the leader. It demonizes foreigners, especially Americans, with a heavy strain of racism and nationalism. This "education" does not stop at graduation because citizens are required to attend weekly study sessions to review North Korean ideology and apply it to their personal lives. Especially in the absence of readily available alternative information, this type of propagandizing society can be effective.

The Kim regime looks for ways to deny its citizens opportunity to oppose the regime and to deter unwanted behavior by threatening punishment. To deny opportunities, the government occupies people's time with mandatory state-led activities. Limiting travel and communication inhibits organizing outside the state in a way that could challenge the regime. To deter, Kim uses repression in the form of punishing those who cross the regime or violate its written or unwritten rules to keep people in line.

Tools of repression include purges and re-education, incarceration, execution, and punishing up to three generations of an offender's family members. Long-term incarcerations, especially in North Korean prison camps, result in notorious levels of deprivation and human rights abuses. Executions are carried out in private and public. Public executions are an explicit attempt to make examples of individuals to deter others from following suit. Punishing children and even grandchildren with long prison sentences for one's behavior gives the regime an ability to impose a punishment worse than death.

How does North Korea propagandize its population?

North Korea propagandizes its people from the cradle to the grave. Regime education begins in the state-run nursery schools and expands considerably as children become old enough to engage the material. Pyongyang inculcates a strong sense of Korean national identity and portrays the Kim family as superhuman heroes defending the Korean nation against foreign imperialists, namely, the United States. Beyond schools, North Korea controls TV and radio broadcast and print media. The news is all regime-controlled and conveys its messages. But the control of mass communications does not end there. The regime creates movies, songs, novels, and public performances to promulgate the values and ideas that support the Kim regime.

North Koreans have little choice but to hear and engage the regime's public line. The government installs radios in homes whose volume can be adjusted, but the user cannot shut them off. Workers are required to attend study sessions to learn more about regime ideology and how it should be applied to current events. They must criticize themselves and their peers for failures to implement this regime guidance in their daily lives. The secret police operate informants throughout society, which makes individuals wary of voicing or sharing any potential skepticism about Pyongyang's claims, even within the nuclear family.

The regime limits access to outside information. Listening to a foreign broadcast such as Voice of America or Radio Free Asia is a punishable offense. So is watching foreign dramas smuggled across the China–North Korea border on DVDs, flash drives, or SD cards. Some North Koreans listen to these foreign broadcasts or watch foreign entertainment, but they do so recognizing that if they get caught, they will have to pay a bribe or risk imprisonment.

The North Korean and Chinese phone systems do not connect, but North Koreans along the northern border can use a Chinese cell phone in North Korea by making calls off the Chinese cell network that bleeds across the border. Those North Koreans living in the far north of the country have made a business off of relaying information to and from the outside world. Those living in other parts of North Korea make calls to someone in the northern part of the country on the North Korea cell phone network. The North Korean living along the Chinese border then makes a separate call off a second, Chinese cell phone operating on the Chinese cell network to convey the messages to those anywhere in the world. In this way, these individuals can relay news from family or friends outside of North Korea for a price.

Chinese cell phones are illegal in North Korea, so people keep conversations short to avoid detection by North Korean monitors. This drives up the cost of such calls and limits the amount of information that can be exchanged.

Some North Koreans can access the Internet under very limited circumstances. If their occupation demands it, some relatively trusted North Koreans can go online in public places.

Monitoring officials and logs of their online activity ensure that they do not access politically inappropriate material. North Koreans cannot access the Internet from home. Even those North Koreans whose jobs requires international communication often share a single email account with others in their work unit, making sure they do not have unauthorized communications over email.

How do North Koreans access outside information?

The North Korean regime has attempted to monopolize mass communications for decades. Restricting access to foreign information allows the regime to control the message to its people, instill ideological values, and propagandize the people without the countervailing influence of contradictory data points. There is always a degree of foreign information seepage in closed societies, but North Korea has managed to maintain a tight lid on information throughout most of its history.

Nonetheless, since the 1990s, the North Korean people have gained relatively greater access to outside information. The information environment is still heavily restricted, and citizens violate the law despite credible promises of severe punishments for accessing illegal information. Nevertheless, North Koreans have increasingly opted to listen to foreign radio broadcasts, watch South Korean or Chinese TV in the border areas, or communicate with friends and family abroad through cell-phone relays.

A survey of North Korean defectors documented some of the means by which North Koreans access outside information beyond the regime's control. The most common method is also the simplest: word of mouth. Friends and family talk with one another and cautiously share information. The advent of markets has in theory provided a venue for discussion, but the regime has recognized this risk and uses human surveillance and informants to limit illicit information exchange.

Another area outside the confines of mass communications is the rise of cell-phone usage. North Korea's cell-phone network is not connected internationally. The phones can only make domestic calls, and North Korean security services make it clear that they have the technical capability to monitor any call. Human informants buttress this capability. Nevertheless, cell phones expand horizontal communications inside North Korea. They also allow greater access to outside information.

North Koreans who live in the country's far north along the Chinese border can also smuggle a Chinese cell phone into North Korea. The Chinese cell towers bleed across the border, making it possible for North Koreans to make international calls on the Chinese network. They can then use their North Korean domestic phones to relay the same information to anywhere in North Korea. The regime's technical surveillance along the border attempts to track and catch those making illegal international calls, so the callers keep the conversations short to avoid detection.

North Korea's legal domestic cell phones can be used in other ways to access foreign information. Though it is illegal to do so, users can insert SD cards into the domestic cell phones and play foreign content like South Korean dramas or music. Entertainment-seeking North Koreans may access this cultural content via smuggled DVDs or USB sticks as well.

South Korean dramas and music are popular in North Korea for their entertainment value, but foreign radio and TV broadcasts also provide real-time information. They can provide the news in a way that movies cannot. North Koreans must smuggle in a basic radio or modify the regime-supplied radio to listen to the foreign broadcasts. US-supported organizations like the Voice of America and Radio Free Asia are the most significant radio broadcasts into North Korea. They offer Korean-language news on a relatively well-resourced platform. A variety of South Korea–based NGOs also broadcast into North Korea, though their listenership is less robust than Voice of America and Radio Free Asia in part because of the technical quality of the broadcasts. The NGO broadcasts also vary considerably in quality of the content of their broadcasts. Some try to discredit the North Korean regime rather than deliver traditional journalism.

Some North Koreans who live in the country's far south can access South Korea television, and some North Koreans in the far north can access Chinese TV. This offers another route to real time information and entertainment.

North Korea heavily restricts access to the Internet. Some privileged individuals can access the Internet from work when their job requires it. Their activity is logged and monitored, leaving little space to access politically incorrect or subversive content. North Korean business leaders or government officials that conduct international work may require basic email access. In this case, the entire office is assigned a single email account to avoid an individual having unbridled communication capabilities with the outside world. North Korea also operates a domestic intranet, but it simply contains state-sanctioned content akin to what is found in the state newspapers, TV, or cultural material.[3]

Do North Koreans have access to cell phones and the Internet?

A sizeable portion of the North Korean population has access to smartphones, while Internet access remains extremely limited. North Korea first experimented with civilian access to cell phones in November 2002, when the North Korean government launched a joint venture with a Thai company. The number of subscribers grew to about twenty thousand through April 2004, when the regime abruptly banned cell-phone use. In April 2004, North Korean leader Kim Jong Il was returning from China by train. Shortly after the train had passed through the Ryongchon station, a massive explosion rocked the area. Kim appeared to consider the explosion an assassination attempt, and there were some reports of a possible cell-phone detonator. The regime responded by banning the devices.

In December 2008, Pyongyang demonstrated renewed interest in allowing its citizens to use cell phones. The 3G technology provided a new way for the regime to keep tabs on user data; the regime could profit from the joint venture; and cell phones could improve business efficiency and quality-of-life for North Korea's elite. In December 2008, the North Korean government again launched a joint venture, this time with Egypt's Orascom. The number of subscribers grew quickly. By 2013, the joint venture reported two million subscribers out of a North Korean population of twenty-four million. By 2017, one estimate placed North Korean cell-phone subscriptions at four million.[4]

North Korean law prevented a single individual from having more than one cell phone, but crafty people could get around this prohibition. By applying for an additional phone in a friend's or family member's name, one person could buy two or more phones. North Korean rate structures made adding additional minutes over the basic allowance more expensive in some cases than buying a second phone, incentivizing the illegal activity of buying multiple phones. This petty crime is most relevant in providing a perspective on the reported four million subscribers. North Korea likely has this number of phones in operation in the country, but less than that number of people actually own them.

The regime was keen to keep close tabs on the technology. They closely watched as the Arab Spring and rise of protests in other parts of the world were fueled by the horizontal communication that cell phones and social media assisted. Pyongyang put in place a series of checks to avoid this same thing affecting their ability to control society. Potential cell-phone users had to apply through the government to access a cell phone. Applicants had to demonstrate a reason for needing a cell phone and the means to pay for it. This provided Pyongyang, in theory, with a way to limit subscribers to the political elite. In practice, applicants could bribe officials, which allowed both the political and newfound business elite to acquire the devices. Once users owned a cell phone, the government made clear to them that it was watching, engaging in transparent surveillance. Smartphone apps showed the user that the government was monitoring their cell phone usage. Even when a user did not connect to the network to use the smartphone to play illicit content, if he or she walked by a hot spot the app would transmit the data to remote surveillance. Police could also stop individuals to check their cell phones, and the regime continued to utilize its extensive network of human informants to keep tabs on citizens. Cell-phone proliferation in North Korea is not a tool for democratizing communications but a means for the regime to monitor and control society.[5]

North Korea's treatment of the Internet is much simpler. It basically prevents individuals from accessing the Internet for personal use. Some people can go online at their workplaces or in universities. However, they must log their activity and demonstrate a reason to access each site, and they are monitored. If the human monitors in the computer lab are insufficient to deter an individual from accessing politically questionable webpages, threat of remote monitoring is enough in most cases to deter user from seeking out illicit sites. North Korean offices that require international communications usually share one communal email account, rather than individual ones, to further limit the possibility of communications contrary to regime objectives.

What are the generational divides in South Korean politics?

North Korea policy is perhaps the most partisan issue in South Korean politics. It is an essential issue of national identity, as well as the overriding national security challenge. It should come as no surprise then that South Koreans take a very close look at North Korea policy and have developed a variety of preferred approaches to North Korea policy. At the broadest level, conservatives tend to prefer a harder line approach to North Korea, are more skeptical of inter-Korean political and economic projects, and prioritize a strong US–South Korean alliance to stand firm against the North Korean threat. South Korean progressives take a softer line. Some progressives consider North Korea not primarily as a threat but as the place where their fellow countrymen live. They favor political and economic engagement, including the provision of aid and joint economic projects to help overcome decades of hostility. Some seek to deprioritize the US–South Korea alliance and focus on the US military presence and political influence in South Korea as an affront to the country's sovereignty.

These two extremes leave ample room for individuals to form their own ideas somewhere in between. Some moderates, for example, favor inter-Korean engagement but worry that Seoul wastes taxpayer money with too generous aid. They may be skeptical that inter-Korean economic projects are helping to resolve the security problems, including the nuclear issue, but they appreciate family reunions and economic projects that seem to make business sense for both sides. Moderates generally support the US–South Korea alliance but not as fervently as the conservatives.

This breakdown of South Korean conservatives, progressives, and moderates follows generational lines. The oldest generation with some connection to the Korean War leans the most conservative. Seeing first-hand the destruction brought by the North Korean invasion in 1950 and appreciation for the US military response at South Korea's most dire hour of need combined to create a generation that favors a strong defense, heavy skepticism of North Korean intentions, and intense support for the United States. Although the generation with first-hand experience of the Korean War is aging and dying off, South Koreans with direct experience with the early Cold War period generally fall into the same camp.

The progressives in South Korea are the middle generation. Whereas in the United States, liberalism is often associated with the youngest group, who become more conservative as they age, this is not the case in South Korea. This 386 generation, named after a computer chip that was well known in the 1990s when the phrase was coined, refers to those who were in their thirties in the 1990s, experienced their defining political moments in the 1980s democratization movement, and were born in the 1960s. Today, this group is approaching middle age, and they remain progressive.

During the 1980s democratization movement, this generation came out in force to protest the conservative military government. They saw the United States as supporting South Korean authoritarianism and being complicit in the military government's human rights abuses. The South Korean government's violent suppression of a protest movement in 1980 in Gwangju, which many progressives believe was perpetrated with Washington's tacit consent, is often labeled as the birth of Korean anti-Americanism. This generation is more skeptical of the United States, including its threat assessment of North Korea. They focus on the shared Korean national identity and sometimes articulate the North Koreans more as "brothers" than enemies. South Korean progressives and conservatives disagree bitterly on the best approach to North Korea.

South Korean moderates are the youngest generation of Koreans and strike a position between those of their parents and grandparents. In a certain sense, they are the least intensely focused on North Korea. They are less likely to support Korean unification, either to rid the peninsula of the DPRK or as an act of national reconciliation. Recognizing North Korea's poverty and underdevelopment, they do not want to limit South Korea's own hard-won economic gains to achieve this objective. They want to avoid war and tensions, which leads them to support certain inter-Korean economic projects, but they shy away from lavishing resources on the North at the expense of South Korean taxpayers and other government domestic spending priorities. They are more likely to favor treating North Korea like any other state rather than as a special case for Seoul's external policy.

What are the geographic divides in South Korean politics?

Korea overwhelmingly is an ethnically homogenous country. It does not have a variety of racial, ethnic, or linguistic groups who provide a basis for political organization in many countries. In theory, this would allow Koreans to focus exclusively on the contest of ideas in national elections, selecting candidates not based on a group identification but wholly based on how closely a candidate aligns with a voter's preference on policy. In practice, the ROK has been beset by regionalism that has affected the country's political and economic development for most of its existence as a modern state.

South Korea can be roughly divided into three regions: the southwest provinces of Cholla, the southeast provinces of Kyongsang, and the northern area of greater Seoul. Cholla tends to vote for progressive candidates, Kyongsang for conservatives, and Seoul tips the balance one way or the other. Some trace the origins of this regionalism as far back as the ancient Korean Three Kingdoms period, but contemporary political divisions require a more proximate explanation.

For better or worse, Koreans have favored local candidates for political office. Those who have graduated from the schools in a given region share critical networks that extend across their careers in business and politics. Politicians have favored their own regions in economic development decisions, a phenomenon common around the world among legislators elected by individual districts, but disproportionately affecting those holding national political office in South Korea, including the presidency.

For example, South Korean president Park Chung-hee, who directed the country's rapid industrialization, hailed from the southeast. This part of the country has many of the natural ports conducive to industry, but Park's concentration of industrial development in the region was stunning. Korea's economic miracle saw new and profitable steel plants, carmakers, and oil refineries pop up in the southeast. The major highways and rail networks also served the region. Those in the country's southwest, whose economy remained primarily agricultural throughout the economic miracle of industrialization, felt left out.

The progressive opposition to Park's conservative rule was concentrated in the southwest Cholla provinces. Korea's most famous progressive dissident and later its president, Kim Dae-jung, came from this part of the country. When Park's successor and the last military leader of South Korea, Chun Doo-hwan, cracked down on democratic protests in 1980, the bloody repression took place in Cholla in the city of Gwangju. A quarter century after South Korea's democratization, these regional affiliations continue to motivate voters. The continuing expansion of the population of Seoul at the expense of the southeast and southwest regions has moderated these regional disparities somewhat, but many voters still retain their hometown affiliations and political leanings even after moving to the capital area.[6]

What is the Korean Wave in South Korea culture?

The Korean Wave, or "Hallyu," refers to the rapid expansion of the popularity of Korean cultural exports that started in the mid-1990s. Most prominently, South Korean pop music and TV dramas gained an international following as "K-pop" took off in China, Japan, and beyond. In music, "boy bands" and "girl groups"—single-sex troupes of young men or women—became especially popular. However, the singer Psy gained the greatest foothold in the United States and Europe following the 2012 release of the song "Gangnam Style." The music video that showcased a horse-riding dance became a dance craze as Psy topped the European and American charts.

Korean TV dramas also grew in popularity, especially in other parts of Asia. Korean actors and directors enjoyed greater international recognition. The Korean government actively sought to promote these cultural exports, exercising soft power abroad. The Korean government has promoted the expansion beyond pop music and TV to more traditional entertainment areas like art, literature, and classical music. Korean food, cosmetics, and even video games have become more prevalent in other parts of Asia and the world.[7]

What unique pressures face South Korean youth?

Young people everywhere face a variety of challenges and pressures as they come of age and look for their place in the world. South Korean youth are no different, but they face some unique pressures. Intensive preparation for university entrance exams motivates South Korean youth beyond a more general focus on education. High school students attend "cram schools" late into the night, and it is not uncommon to hear of students disregarding their day school's class materials to use the class time to study independently for the standardized test.

Ambitious students in a variety of countries focus intensely on university admissions, but the phenomenon is particularly pronounced in South Korea. Seventy percent of South Koreans under the age of thirty-four have attained a college degree, more than any other country in the world. By way of comparison, 48 percent of Americans and 43 percent of citizens in other developed countries, on average, attain this level of education.[8] The "testing hell," as the university admissions exam preparation is referred to in South Korea, affects a broader segment of youth in South Korea than other countries.

South Korean students and their parents believe, with good reason, that the university they attend will affect their lifelong employment prospects. South Korean big businesses recruit from the select universities. When one considers this, coupled with the fact that South Korean big business offers little opportunity for movement between companies later in one's career, as is common in the West, in favor of a (near-) lifelong employment structure, one can begin to understand why students obsess about the entrance exam. For many South Korean youth, the exam seems to determine their lifelong fate. Employers often prefer a student with poor academic performance at a top college over a top student from what is considered a second-tier institution. Entrance to a select university, not successful academic performance at that institution, is paramount.

South Korea's economy has revolutionized since the 1960s as the country shifted out of poverty to become an advanced industrialized economy. The "economic miracle" created a small number of large companies, which continue to dominate the South Korean economy today. Unlike in the United States, where small businesses and entrepreneurship are appealing routes for many, employment at small and medium-sized businesses in South Korea is considered less prestigious, and wages are significantly lower than those offered by big business.

South Korean students and their parents are well aware of the rigidity of South Korea's testing-education-employment pipeline. Students who do not score as well as they hoped on the university entrance exam may take off a year to study for the test more and try again and again. The pressure is intense and consequences are real. As well as having the highest college graduation rate among the world's developed countries, South Korea has dueled with Lithuania in the last decade for the tragic distinction of being the developed country with the highest suicide rate.[9]

How are North Korean defectors received in South Korea?

North Korean defectors arriving in South Korea enjoy generous government support but often report feelings of discrimination and the disappointment of unmet expectations. The

South Korean government provides North Korean defectors resettling in South Korea with training, subsidized housing and healthcare, financial support, and special admission to South Korea's competitive universities. However, North Korean defectors as a group tend to have a difficult time finding high-paying jobs or newfound social status in the South.

When they arrive in South Korea, defectors go through a security screening and then a mandatory in-residence program to teach them about South Korean society. Hanawon, as the in-residence center is called, provides psychological counseling as well, since many defectors faced trauma in their journey out of North Korea or in their former lives in North Korea. They learn to use an ATM and about other aspects of South Korea's modern society that are absent in the North.

Upon completing the Hanawon program, the defectors are eligible for housing and medical-care support, job training, and preferred admission to South Korean universities. The South Korean government tries to give them the tools to succeed in South Korea's hyper-competitive society. However, defectors still have a difficult time achieving the level of social and economic success they may have envisioned before leaving North Korea. Defectors appear to face discrimination as well as an underdevelopment of skills highly valued in the South Korean marketplace and society that their South–Korea-born counterparts have been honing much longer.

North Korean defectors also report harassment and discrimination in South Korea too. They speak the same language but have a discernible accent. They report facing assumptions that they lack the same work ethic as native-born South Koreans. In other words, some South Koreans assume that they are relatively lazy. Few have gotten rich in South Korea, and a small handful have even returned to North Korea, noting their disappointment in advancing their personal livelihoods in the South. The defectors are undoubtedly better off in South Korea on material metrics, but they do not resemble the fashionable and well-off South Koreans that popularize South Korean dramas that are found in the North. The South Korean government wants to see the defectors succeed, report their success to others in North Korea, and encourage more defections. However, defectors' social mobility so far remains limited.

11

NORTH KOREAN HUMAN RIGHTS

What is the status of human rights in North Korea?

North Korea has perhaps the worst human rights record on the planet today. Human rights abuses have been severe since the origins of the country, and such abuses are an institutionalized and structural element of the regime.

The Kim family stays in power through a series of repressive measures and cooptation. The regime punishes those who cross it and rewards those who support it. It systematically prejudges loyalty by one's family background, sorting individuals from birth into different classes that afford or limit their educational access and future job prospects, social standing, healthcare, housing quality, and wealth.

Every country attempts to condition its citizens' behavior for a social good. Murder is outlawed everywhere, and states seek to discourage a crime all can easily agree is against the social good. Different countries have more controversial laws that more clearly expose that law is based on a common idea of morality in a country. For example, France's valuing secularism has led it to effectively ban Muslim girls from wearing headscarves to public schools, and Singapore's strong opposition to drug use has prompted severe punishments, including the death penalty, for drug traffickers. Each nation claims its own right to determine its internal affairs in accordance with its own particular moral understanding. North Korea values most highly loyalty to the leader. This is a basic part of the regime's moral code, so offenses deemed threatening to the North Korean leader or regime face the greatest punishment. North Korea claims this is their prerogative and that other states should not interfere in its internal affairs. However, the United Nations Charter recognizes certain basic human rights ascribed to the individual that states cannot violate. North Korea is a member of the United Nations and has agreed to uphold human rights, but these basic principles apply to all states regardless of membership in the world body. North Korea's basic mode of conditioning its citizens' behavior systematically violates their most basic human rights.

Human rights abuses are most easily seen in repression. If a North Korean citizen crosses into China illegally and returns, state authorities can arrest the individual and sentence him or her to prison for illegal border crossing. Those who interact with Christian missionaries while in China, though, receive an even stiffer punishment over those engaged in simple cross-border trade. Pyongyang associates Christianity with the West and Protestant and Evangelical Christian missionaries, in particular, with conservative South Korean groups opposed to the North Korean regime. Consequently, the same illegal border crossers who carried ideas that the regime fears may undermine its political control are met with harsh sentences.

The Kim regime also punishes family members of "criminals." For example, if one person defects to South Korea, his or her family members back in North Korea can be sent to a sprawling prison camp for a life of hard labor. North Korea allows for the punishment of up to three generations, meaning a young child and his or her parents can be sentenced to life in a prison camp for an offense committed by the child's grandparent. It is a perverse set of punishments that not only utilizes the death penalty extensively but seeks punishments beyond death by credibly threatening one's children and grandchildren as well.

North Korea's human rights abuses are not limited to repression; its effort to co-opt citizens actually produces human rights abuses too. For example, the regime has historically controlled the distribution of the basic necessities of life such as food and medicine. The politically loyal get prioritized access, meaning the regime channels scarce food and medicine away from those who may need it most to reward the politically loyal. The state's denying its citizens basic necessities in this way constitutes a human rights violation.

North Korea's emphasis on loyalty to the leader is central to its political identity and the basic functioning of government. It is difficult to see how the regime could abandon these severe human rights abuses without a wholesale revolution of its system of governance. Indeed, many of the North Korean human rights activists operating in South Korea openly support regime change, arguing the Kim regime could never fundamentally reject human rights abuses, thus, ending the Kim dynasty is a moral imperative. In turn, North Korea says that human rights activists are just trying to disguise their true intent to overturn the Kim regime's rule and are making up lies about human rights violations in North Korea.

Other human rights activists dispute the feasibility or desirability of North Korean regime change. They advocate a process of steadily improving North Korean human rights, beginning with improving unprivileged North Koreans' access to food and medicine or providing assistance to North Korea's disabled populace and orphans. This group favors humanitarian assistance as a general rule over "naming and shaming" the Kim regime's human rights abuses. While North Korea vilifies the first group, the second group depends on the regime's cooperation to try to help the North Korean people. South Korean civil society focused on North Korea's human rights and humanitarian situation is polarized between these two camps.

What was the UN's Commission of Inquiry?

The UN's Commission of Inquiry was the most significant multilateral effort to hold North Korea to account for its human rights abuses to date. The UN Charter (1945) and UN Universal Declaration of Human Rights (1948) lay out the expectation that all UN member states will respect and uphold "the inherent dignity and of the equal and inalienable rights of all members of the human family" as a fundamental precept.[1] States are sovereign and can mind their own internal affairs, but this does not grant them free rein to trample on the basic human dignity of their citizens. North Korea acceded to these precepts when it joined the United Nations in 1991 and had a certain obligation to uphold them even before its voluntary decision to join the world body.

National governments like the United States, regional groupings like the European Union, and major international NGOs like Human Rights Watch and Amnesty International have long criticized North Korea's human rights record and called for it to improve its practices. In 2003, the UN human rights body issued its first resolution criticizing North Korea's human rights record and urging it to cooperate with UN representatives to improve both the rights situation and the country's access to humanitarian relief.[2] North Korea refused to acknowledge the legitimacy of the vote, and it even retaliated against the European Union by calling off a human rights dialogue with the regional body after the EU sponsored the resolution.

The UN human rights body and the UN General Assembly continued to pass resolutions condemning North Korea's human rights record with increasing numbers of supporting countries. The UN established a Special Rapporteur to investigate North Korean abuses, but the poorly resourced official could do little and never gained access to North Korea. Human rights activists started calling for a UN Commission of Inquiry (COI), which would have more resources to investigate North

Korea's human rights conditions, file a comprehensive report to shed more light on the topic, and suggest further international action to redress the dire state of North Korean human rights. In 2013, the composition of the UN Human Rights Council was favorable for such a vote, and the UN body authorized the COI.

The UN Commission of Inquiry was led by an internationally respected jurist, Michael Kirby. Kirby had previously worked as a justice on Australia's High Court, and he employed a small team of investigators who cooperated with a variety of actors to investigate North Korean abuses. The investigation lasted a year, but North Korea refused Kirby access to the country and continued to criticize the legitimacy of the probe. The COI produced a 372-page report, detailing its findings.[3]

The COI determined that North Korea's human rights abuses are so severe that they constitute "crimes against humanity." It referred the matter to the UN Security Council. The Security Council has authority to impose more consequential punishments, including referring individual human rights abusers like Kim Jong Un to the International Criminal Court for prosecution. However, China is a permanent member of the Security Council with a veto and was widely expected to block any such move. The UN Human Rights Council did pass the matter to the UN Security Council, which even held rare sessions on the human rights topic, but the matter did not go further. The COI exposed and documented North Korean human rights abuses in a way unprecedented by the world body and encouraged more states to pressure North Korea on the topic, but it did not perceptibly improve North Korea's conduct toward its people.

What are North Korea's prison camps?

North Korea's penal system operates traditional jails and prisons as well as expansive labor camps in remote parts of the country, where inmates serve long-term incarcerations. The prison camps are the sites of some of North Korea's most notorious human rights abuses. Credible estimates place the prison camp population at around two hundred thousand people.

North Korea publicly acknowledges it has a penal system, long-term incarcerations, and sentences of "hard labor." However, it denies perpetrating any rights abuses and maintains that the conduct of its prison system is wholly an internal, sovereign matter. Foreign nations and international bodies like the United Nations have no place to criticize North Korea's penal system, they claim.

The existence of North Korea's prison camps and the extensive human rights violations that occur there is well documented. Serious and nonpartisan organizations, such as the Database Center for North Korean Human Rights, have corroborated numerous accounts of public executions, forced abortions, beatings and torture, denial of necessities of life like adequate food and medicine, and cross-generational punishments. North Korea punishes not only the individual, who violates certain laws or otherwise crosses the state, but also up to three generations of his or her kin. Consequently, a child can be imprisoned in a prison camp for his or her grandparent's transgression.

Though satellite imagery has further demonstrated the existence of these camps, most of the harrowing tales of rights abuses come from former inmates who defect from North Korea after being released from a camp. Though many people sent to prison camps never emerge alive, some are released after serving their sentences. Many North Korean defectors have told their stories to public audiences, national authorities, and UN commissions. One man, Shin Dong-hyuk, escaped from a North Korean prison and shared his story with a noted Western journalist, Blaine Harden; the resulting book was a *New York Times* best seller.[4]

North Korea slanders and threatens defectors who share their experiences with prison camps as politically motivated liars. Pyongyang denies committing rights abuses while also refusing international human rights bodies to access named prisons. The North Korean government notes that the defectors are hostile to the Kim regime or paid puppets of South Korea or the United States. They claim the defectors' "lies" are only efforts to bring down the regime.

Indeed, many North Korean defectors, especially prison camp survivors, oppose the Kim regime. Some even argue that the only way to end the human rights abuses that are a fundamental part of the regime's ability to control society is to overthrow Kim. It would take a saintly capacity for forgiveness for a former inmate to feel and act differently. But this does not mean their accounts are wrong. It is common for survivors of extreme trauma to get some facts wrong in retelling their stories, and some high-profile errors have fed the North Korean effort to discredit all defector testimony. However, the overall assessment of a body of evidence is unmistakable: North Korea severely abuses human rights in its prison camps.

Are North Koreans really starving?

North Koreans face chronic malnutrition, and the least politically connected and most vulnerable groups bear the worst of it. "Chronic malnutrition" is the technical term used by the UN World Food Programme and the Food and Agriculture Organization (FAO). It means that millions of North Koreans do not get a proper diet. They especially do not get enough proteins to be healthy, such as meat and fish. The problem is "chronic," because it is a long-standing issue that is not going away.

The most vulnerable groups include pregnant women, babies and children, the sick, and the elderly. Those with political connections, such members of the Korean Workers' Party, government officials, and military officers, do relatively well. Those who work in prioritized state sectors, farming (and therefore have direct access to some of their own food production) or who trade in local markets to make money also do better than others. But those too young, old, sick, or not politically connected make up the vulnerable groups.

International aid groups in North Korea seek to help the vulnerable groups. They do not seek to feed the whole population or even make up the country's entire food shortfall. These aid groups take great pains to ensure the regime cannot divert this aid to the North Korean military or elites. The provision of items like baby formula and non-rice foodstuffs that are less palatable to elites and the use of a variety of technical monitoring and delivery strategies help ensure international aid goes to the intended recipients.

Compared to South Korea's wealth, the North Korean government's inability—or unwillingness—to prioritize feeding its own population is stunning. Unfortunately, North Korea's level of food insecurity is common. North Korea ranks in the middle of Asian countries on food insecurity metrics, according to the FAO. The prevalence of stunting among children, where insufficient nutrition impedes normal growth, is famous in North Korea. South Koreans are inches taller than their North Korean counterparts. However, North Korea's prevalence of stunting is marginally better than the average in the Asia Pacific region.[5] During the late 1990s famine, North Korea's food situation was extraordinarily bad, but the food situation has moderated since then. It is not great, but it is not the worst in the world by a long stretch.

The most tragic element of North Korean hunger is that it is largely preventable. North Korea grows most of its own food even though the mountainous country has little suitable arable land. It also accepts international food aid and imports some food as well. Even during the greatest North Korean food deficits during the famine, the regime actually decreased its food imports when it received international aid. Even though its people's food needs were far from met by the aid, the Kim regime opted to put its money elsewhere. Despite aid organizations' robust monitoring to ensure that food goes to its intended recipients, aid creates a moral hazard risk that Pyongyang will simply buy less food from abroad as it gets more free food from the aid organizations.

Foreign officials often lambast the regime's decisions to invest in costly defense systems or grandiose prestige projects while nonprioritized groups inside North Korea lack basics like food and medicine. While this is true, Pyongyang does not have to choose between rockets and rice—national security and food security. Modestly curtailing the aggressive prioritization of the expensive nuclear and missile programs could purchase many food imports to feed the North Korean population.

Traditionally, feeding all of the North Korean people simply has not been a high regime priority as judged by where the regime actually puts its money. However, one glimmer of hope is Kim Jong Un's public pronouncements on improving the livelihoods of North Koreans. Since Kim Jong Un's coming to power in 2011, the regime has spent more on commercial food imports. In 2010, Kim Jong Il's North Korea spent $154 million on imported foodstuffs; in 2017, Kim Jong Un's North Korea almost doubled that number, to $296 million.[6]

What is the "right to food"?

The right to food stems from a basic premise: people must eat to survive. Consequently, taking actions that actively deny a group of people the ability to survive in this way constitutes a human rights violation. The UN Commission of Inquiry evaluating North Korea's human rights situation specifically investigated whether the North Korean government denied groups of its people their right to food for political ends. It determined that North Korea did deny this human right.

North Korea prioritizes resources based largely on political loyalty. Those from trusted families get better access to education, housing, career opportunities, medical care—and food. Traditionally, the North Korean regime directly distributed food through a state system called the Public Distribution System. Although this system broke down during the 1990s famine and was later reconstituted, local markets have played an increasing role in distributing goods, including some food items, in North Korea. Nonetheless, the regime has its hand in every stage of food production, import, or aid solicitation and delivery. Elites still worry least about food access. The regime's political prioritization of certain groups over others to the point of depriving the disadvantaged a basic subsistence amounts to a violation of the human rights of the politically disaffected.

More hopefully, greater international acceptance of food as a fundamental human right helps bridge the sharply divided civil society organizations committed to "North Korean human rights" and "North Korea's humanitarian situation." The "human rights" activists tend to take a harder line on the Kim regime, criticizing its despicable actions like the treatment of those in prison camps. The "humanitarian" groups seek to provide food, medicine, and education to the North Korean people and must work with the Kim regime to gain access to the country. This second group tends to take a softer line approach to public criticism of Kim as a result. The two groups are critical of each other because their approaches contrast even if their goals may be similar with respect to improving life for the North Korean people.

Recognizing that both groups seek to advance human rights can help forge creative areas of collaboration. For example, North Korea's prison camps, which are often a core focus of the human rights groups, leave prisoners with inadequate food and medicine. Beyond the young, old, sick and unemployed, North Korean prisoners also face a dire situation. Humanitarian groups conversant in food and medicine deliveries seeking to add prisoners as a target group could be one way to tangibly improve, even if not solve, the horrible plight of North Korea's prisoners.

Further, if food is a right, providing it to vulnerable groups is addressing directly a regime abuse of human rights. It does not provide accountability for the violator, but takes a victim-centered approach. Some aid critics argue that food aid props up the rights-abusing Kim regime; withholding aid, they maintain, could hasten its downfall. Greater international understanding of the right to food makes this argument harder to make. Food cannot be used as a political weapon by any side without committing human rights violations. Food aid can be debated on its humanitarian merits, but it is inappropriate to use food to advance political goals.

Why does North Korea target Christians in particular for persecution?

North Korea's constitution guarantees religious freedom, but the regime denies its people this right in practice. Pyongyang is hostile to the practice of all religions, but it persecutes Protestant and Evangelical Christians above others. Since the DPRK's founding in 1948, the Kim dynasty has been wary of Christians, whom it associates with the West and South Korea. The first South Korean president, Syngman Rhee, was educated by Christian missionaries in Korea before moving to the United States for much of the Japanese colonial period and returning to South Korea in 1945 as a fervent anticommunist. Kim Il Sung purged the factions in North Korea with ties to foreign powers, including Russia and China, as well as individuals with some semblance of loyalty to South Korea or Christianity. Kim Il Sung's consolidation of power sought to remove as a potential political threat anyone with an allegiance to another, including to God.

Christianity has thrived in South Korea; red neon crosses dot the night skyline and people are commonly found evangelizing on the street in downtown Seoul. However, Protestant and Evangelical Christianity has developed with a more politically conservative bent, while Catholic Christians played a greater role in the democratization movement and profess a more liberal political outlook. Today, Protestant and Evangelical Christians continue to take a harder line on North Korea, while Catholics continue to favor engagement. Conservative South Korean president Lee Myung-bak was an influential leader in a South Korean Protestant megachurch; liberal South Korean presidents Kim Dae-jung and Moon Jae-in were Catholic.

Fairly or not, North Korea associates Protestant and Evangelical Christians with elements hostile to it and potentially even supporters of regime change. North Korea has loosened some elements of its persecution of Christians during its history. For example, it allowed four churches to be built in Pyongyang, and Kim Il Sung received a famous American evangelist, Billy Graham, in North Korea with great fanfare. However, the regime still doles out much more severe punishments for those caught returning from China if they had contact with Christians while over the border than for those who simply engaged in illegal cross-border trade. The Kim regime severely punishes foreigners as well who leave a Bible for others to find or otherwise engage in the slightest hint of evangelizing.

Beyond fear of Christian groups potentially hostile to the Kim regime, North Korea expends great effort to instill in its population an unmitigated loyalty to the Kim family. North Korean state ideology does not have space for loyalty to God as well as Kim. Further, it is conceivable that the Kim dynasty has likewise taken a lesson from modern Chinese history. In the mid-nineteenth century, a Chinese man who believed himself to be the younger brother of Jesus Christ initiated a massive revolt called the Taiping Rebellion. The fervor in the rebellion led to full-scale civil war that claimed the lives of tens of millions of Chinese. The Kim regime had little reason to risk allowing such ideas into the country, and it has stamped out Christianity in North Korea with vigor.

12

THE FUTURE

What are the prospects for Korean unification?

The near-term prospects for Korean unification are dim, but unification remains a constitutionally derived, foundational idea of the ROK and DPRK that makes its eventual realization possible. Korean nationalism is strong on both sides of the DMZ. North Korea is more intense in its violently aggressive nationalism and demonization of foreigners; South Korea is more globalized, but it is still resistant to significant inflows of immigrants that could undercut the country's ethnic homogeneity. While Americans may articulate the country's diversity as a core asset, North and South Koreans traditionally have presented the reverse—that unity drives their society. Koreans often see the peninsula's division as unfortunate and unnatural, creating a push for unification that has continued at varying levels of intensity for seven decades.

Politics has gotten in the way of unification. The DPRK and ROK agreed from the outset that unifying the Korean people in one homeland was paramount. However, both governments saw that as their destiny, and the other government as standing as a barrier to achieving this right and just singular Korea. Inter-Korean reconciliation efforts have had some notable successes in limited areas. For example, the two Koreas have fielded a unified Korean team in multiple international sporting events, most recently, at the 2018 Winter Olympics. Fusing a women's Olympic hockey team is easier than finding a unification formula for two polar opposite political, economic, and social systems. The two sides have seriously explored various political proposals to unify since the 1970s. Both sides effectively have a special ministry dedicated to promoting unification, but the work continues. Unification may well come in the medium-to-long-term, because the Korean nation wants one country. But until there is greater agreement on what that unified country looks like, the peninsula's division is likely to stay.

Will North Korea ever denuclearize?

Maybe. North Korea has pledged multiple times and has, on occasion, taken verifiable and irreversible steps toward denuclearization. However, the nuclear problem is still with us because past diplomatic efforts have not achieved North Korea's complete denuclearization.

The North Korean nuclear issue is so hard that many analysts say denuclearization is simply out of reach. North Korea relies on its nuclear arsenal to deter a feared US invasion to topple the regime. Given the priority of protecting Kim and his regime, Pyongyang would never trade away the world's most powerful weapon, these analysts claim. Others maintain there may be a narrow path to denuclearization. If North Korea can gain an alternative means to security by limiting the United States military footprint in South Korea and get some economic benefits to boot, there may be an opportunity for hard choices on both sides to craft a workable denuclearization deal. The US–North Korea summit in Singapore on June 12, 2018, sketched out these general trade-offs as the vision of the two leaders, Donald Trump and Kim Jong Un. The follow-on diplomatic process will test whether Kim Jong Un is a different kind of North Korean leader and whether denuclearization may be attainable.

Will South Korea develop nuclear weapons?

South Korea had a nuclear weapons program in the 1970s, and public opinion polls in recent years show majority South Korean support for its own nuclear weapons program today. However, a string of South Korean presidential administrations has pledged that they will not develop nuclear weapons because it would severely damage the US–South Korea alliance and the South Korean economy.

In the 1970s, South Korea's military government pursued nuclear weapons. Seoul worried that Washington was withdrawing from Asia. President Richard Nixon in 1969 called on Asian states to provide for more of their own security, naming South Vietnam primarily but also mentioning South Korea. After the United States withdrew its troops from Vietnam, North Vietnam wiped South Vietnam off the map, reunified the country, and tortured and executed many of the former South Vietnamese leaders. When United States withdrew one-third of its troops from South Korea in 1971, and President Jimmy Carter pursued a complete withdrawal of US troops in South Korea for most of his 1977–1981 term, Seoul was worried about the United States abandoning it. Facing a superior military force in North Korea that South Korea did not believe it could stop without American help, Seoul pursued its own nuclear weapons.

The United States learned about its ally's secret nuclear weapons program and pressured South Korea to end it. The United States did not want to see an escalation of the nuclear arms race on the Korean Peninsula or in the world. The nonproliferation regime established by the United States and the Soviet Union in 1968 to stop the spread of nuclear weapons to new powers had global implications. If South Korea could develop nuclear weapons with impunity, what would stop Japan or Saudi Arabia from following suit? South Korea decided to end its nuclear weapons program in 1979, shortly before the assassination of South Korean president Park Chung-hee. Park's successor finished off the last remnants of the nuclear program as President Ronald Reagan came to power in Washington and pledged a more robust defense relationship with Seoul. Two and a half decades later, after South Korean democracy had been consolidated, the idea of a South Korean nuclear weapon came back in vogue. By the mid-2000s, North Korea had advanced its nuclear weapons and missile programs to such an extent that strategic thinkers and politicians in South Korea started talking again about the implications in the not-too-distant future of North Korea being able to strike the United States with nuclear weapons. Some South Koreans feared that if North Korea could credibly hold at risk the American homeland, Washington may be less likely to come to Seoul's defense as promised in a crisis. With a credible threat to the American backing, Seoul would need nuclear weapons to deter North Korea, they argued. Simpler versions of the argument held that if North Korea had nuclear weapons, South Korea should be able to have them too.

Polls taken shortly after North Korea's first and second nuclear tests, in 2006 and 2009, respectively, showed majority support in South Korea for its own nuclear weapons program. The timing of the polls may have bolstered support rates, but the country had not yet had a full conversation about the costs and benefits of such a fateful decision. The American and South Korean governments publicly declared their opposition to a South Korean nuclear weapon. Such a weapon was unnecessary given the strength of the US–South Korean alliance, including the extension of the US nuclear umbrella. A South Korean nuclear weapon would violate the country's own international commitments, risking escalation on the peninsula and off. It would require that South Korea withdraw from the landmark 1968 Nuclear Nonproliferation Treaty (NPT), placing it in the company of the one other country to have ever done so: North Korea.

North Korea endured international isolation and sanctions for its nuclear quest. It hardly provides an attractive model for other states, but South Korea pursuing nuclear weapons with impunity may prompt other states to reconsider whether they really needed to forgo nuclear weapons too. If South Korea were to embark on a nuclear weapons quest, it would lose the moral high ground and international legitimacy it earned in calling for decades for peninsula-wide denuclearization.

North Korea would certainly cry foul if its nuclear pursuit and NPT withdrawal led to crippling economic sanctions and international isolation but South Korea's did not. As a world-class trading state, South Korea's facing possible sanctions or even international investors distancing themselves from the country would have profound economic consequences. Given the full stakes, it is not surprising that every South Korean government since Park Chung-hee has foresworn nuclear weapons, and this is likely to continue.

Will North Korea liberalize its economy?

The North Korean government has allowed a modest amount of economic liberalization, since the mid-1990s famine in particular. Liberalization proceeds in fits and starts, but the North Korean state remains highly involved in the economy. There is much more room to liberalize than to move in the opposite direction, and North Korean leader Kim Jong Un has already extended this basic liberalization effort. This modest liberalization effort is likely to continue and expand.

Whether North Korea decides to fundamentally transform its autarkic economic ways emphasizing self-sufficiency and make the necessary political decisions to reform and open up is more difficult to predict. To put the ambitious economic reform model in perspective, North Korea watchers debate whether North Korea could reach the levels of economic liberalization found in China or Vietnam. Both the Chinese and Vietnamese economic reforms produced tremendous economic growth for both countries, raised many people out of poverty, and allowed the communist parties in both countries to retain power. These markets remain illiberal owing to undue government intervention, corruption impacting foreign trade, and discriminatory treatment of foreign firms. North Korea's economy is so much more illiberal than this that reaching the China or Vietnam model is held out as the gold standard of possible North Korean economic liberalization efforts.

Kim Jong Un has pursued some economic reforms that incentivize increased domestic production, and he officially penned a summit agreement with President Donald Trump to seek sanctions relief, among other things, to encourage foreign trade and investment. While Kim Jong Un has not outlined an ambitious economic reform plan like China's or Vietnam's, he is likely to try to improve his country's economic lot on the margins by boosting domestic efficiency and loosening some restrictions on foreign trade.

Will North Korea ever improve its human rights record?

Unfortunately, human rights violations are a systemic problem in North Korea. One can and should advocate for improved human rights conditions with real impact on people's lives, but it is difficult to see North Korea ceasing to be a rights-violating regime without revolution, regime change, or unification.

The Kim family's ability to control North Korean politics and society uses carrots and sticks that violate rights. It doles out privilege based on the Songbun classification system. Affording the elite much better access to food, for example, because their families are considered more politically loyal, denies those at the bottom of the social classification system enough to eat based on their perceived disloyalty. The regime uses food as a weapon and violates rights. This is not an aberration or out of the norm in North Korea; rather, rights violations are part and parcel of the system.

Likewise, the Kim regime relies on repression to deny its citizens access to "subversive" information like Voice of America or Radio Free Asia broadcasts and deters unwanted behavior by threatening punishment. The horrors of its penal system, including public executions, seek to credibly show the North Korean people that crossing the regime has severe consequences. While the regime could release individual political prisoners and improve the notoriously abysmal situation in prison camps, it would require a more fundamental political transformation to end rights-abusing repression wholesale.

Some of the NGOs in South Korea focused on the human rights abuses, especially those led by North Korean defectors, call for regime change. They argue that the Kim regime will always violate rights until it is brought down. Other NGOs tend to prefer making whatever improvements possible on specific cases of human rights abuses in North Korea. They note that a military effort to end the regime would create even more death and destruction, so they look for opportunities to advance rights peacefully wherever they can.

Both groups are correct in some respects of their analysis. Peaceful human rights advocacy can have effect on the margins. Those margins are human lives, so it is a worthwhile endeavor. But this advocacy is not likely to fundamentally transform North Korea's human-rights-abusing behavior without a political revolution in the country. The most sustainable resolution of the North Korean security threat and rights abuses is unification, making this long-term Korean effort more than a question of nationalism but a critically important one to foreign nations and humanitarians as well.

Who will lead North Korea after Kim Jong Un?

North Korea's constitution has no provision for hereditary succession. Kim Il Sung's selection of his eldest son to succeed him was a personal and extraconstitutional move. Kim Jong Il's tapping his third son to follow him was the same. Since Kim Jong Un came to power relatively recently, in December 2011, and his age (born 1983) raises the possibility of his remaining in power for decades more, there has been little discussion of who may follow Kim Jong Un.

Kim Jong Un's polity appears outwardly stable, but human life is always fragile. Kim Jong Un's extraordinary weight gain while in office has been the butt of jokes, but morbid obesity raises serious health consequences. What happens if Kim Jong Un suddenly dies because of chronic health conditions or a freak accident? He has not yet designated or groomed an obvious heir. His children are not yet in elementary school. The one family member Kim Jong Un has empowered with an important office and duties is his younger sister, Kim Yo Jong. She was his personal representative at the 2018 Winter Olympics in South Korea that pushed forward the inter-Korean summit with President Moon Jae-in. She also traveled with her older brother to Singapore for the first ever US–North Korea summit.

Kim Yo Jong is a woman in a country not too familiar with female political leaders, but she already exercises significant political power. Critically, she's also a Kim. The Kim regime has propagated the importance of the Kim family bloodline for most of North Korean history. Someone other than a member of the Kim family ruling North Korea would be far more jarring to North Korean politics than a woman at the helm. If Kim Jong Un dies tomorrow, Kim Yo Jong may very well be the first female North Korean heir. If he survives longer, Kim will get the chance to designate his own preference and signal this to his country and the world like his father and grandfather did.

NOTES

Chapter 1

1. Carter Eckert, Ki-baik Lee, Young Ick Lee, Michael Robinson, and Edward Wagner, *Korea Old and New: A History* (Seoul and Cambridge, MA: Ilchokak and Harvard University Press, 1990).
2. United Nations, UN Security Council Resolutions 83–84 (1950), http://www.un.org/en/ga/search/view_doc.asp?symbol=S/RES/84(1950).
3. United States Forces Korea, "United Nations Command," accessed June 1, 2018, http://www.usfk.mil/About/United-Nations-Command/.
4. B. R. Myers, *The Cleanest Race: How North Koreans See Themselves and Why It Matters* (Brooklyn, NY: Melville House, 2011).
5. "Telegram from Kuznetsov and Fedorenko in Pyongyang," March 29, 1953, History and Public Policy Program Digital Archive, AVPRF, Fond 059a, Opis 5a, Delo 5, Papka 11, Listy 120–22, https://digitalarchive.wilsoncenter.org/document/112123.
6. "Korean War Armistice," Wilson Center Digital Archive, accessed June 5, 2018, http://digitalarchive.wilsoncenter.org/collection/169/korean-war-armistice.

Chapter 2

1. "North Korean Purges—Kim Il-sung," GlobalSecurity.org, accessed July 25, 2018, https://www.globalsecurity.org/military/world/dprk/leadership-purges.htm.
2. Andrei Lankov, "Soviet-DPRK Relations: Purges, Power, and Dissent in North Korea's Formative Years," *SinoNK*, March 29,

2013, https://sinonk.com/2013/03/29/lankov-on-ussr-DPRK-50s-60s/.

3. Chen Jian, "North Korea's Relations with China," Wilson Center Digital Archive, Modern Korean History Portal, accessed July 25, 2018, http://digitalarchive.wilsoncenter.org/resource/modern-korean-history-portal/north-korea-s-relations-with-china.

4. U.S. Department of State, *American Foreign Policy 1950–1955: Basic Documents, Department of State Publication 6446, General Foreign Policy Series 117* (Washington, DC: U.S. Government Printing Office, 1957), "Mutual Defense Treaty between the United States and the Republic of Korea," signed October 1, 1953, ratifications exchanged and entered into force on November 17, 1954, Yale Law School Avalon Project, http://avalon.law.yale.edu/20th_century/kor001.asp.

5. Ibid.

6. Victor Cha, *Powerplay: The Origins of the American Alliance System in Asia* (Princeton, NJ: Princeton University Press, 2016), 94–121.

7. "Mutual Defense Treaty between the United States and the Republic of Korea," signed October 1, 1953, ratifications exchanged and entered into force on November 17, 1954, Yale Law School Avalon Project, http://avalon.law.yale.edu/20th_century/kor001.asp.

8. World Bank data is priced in current US dollars, adjusted for inflation. "GDP per capita (current US$): Korea, Republic of," World Bank Open Data, accessed June 6, 2018, https://data.worldbank.org/indicator/NY.GDP.PCAP.CD?end=1979&locations=KR&start=1961&view=chart.

9. For a review of some of the economic dynamics at play, see Seoghoon Kang, "Globalization and Income Inequality in South Korea: An Overview," OECD Development Centre paper, December 2001, http://www.oecd.org/dev/2698445.pdf.

10. "Major Indicators Comparison, Per Capita GNI," Bank of Korea, accessed June 6, 2018, https://ecos.bok.or.kr/flex/EasySearch_e.jsp. The Bank of Korea is South Korea's central bank.

11. Michael Lerner and Jong-dae Shin, "New Romanian Evidence on the Blue House Raid and the *USS Pueblo* Incident," North Korea International Documentation Project, April 20, 2012, Wilson Center, https://www.wilsoncenter.org/publication/new-romanian-evidence-the-blue-house-raid-and-the-uss-pueblo-incident.

12. Hannah Fischer, *North Korean Provocative Actions, 1950–2007* (Washington, DC: Congressional Research Service, 2007).
13. Ibid.
14. "The July 4 North-South Joint Communique," United Nations Peacemaker Document Retrieval, July 4, 1972, http:// peacemaker.un.org/korea-4july-communique72.
15. See Henry Kissinger, *On China* (New York: Penguin, 2012), chap. 9.
16. See William Keylor, *The Twentieth Century World: An International History* (Oxford: Oxford University Press, 1996), 317–381.
17. Richard Nixon, "Address to the Nation on the War in Vietnam," November 3, 1969, https://www.nixonfoundation.org/2017/09/ address-nation-war-vietnam-november-3-1969/.
18. Kang Choi and Joon-sung Park, "South Korea: Fears of Abandonment and Entrapment," in *The Long Shadow: Nuclear Weapons and Security in 21st Century Asia*, ed. Muthiah Alagappa (Stanford, CA: Stanford University Press, 2008), 373–403.
19. CIA, "Rangoon Bombing Incident: The Case against the North Koreans," October 19, 1983, Declassified July 2000, https://www. cia.gov/library/readingroom/docs/DOC_0000408056.pdf.
20. For a more detailed account of Nordpolitik, see Tae Dong Chung, "Korea's Nordpolitik: Achievements and Prospects," *Asian Perspective* 15, no. 2 (Fall–Winter 1991): 149–178.
21. Aidan Foster-Carter, "A Long and Winding Road: South Korea's 'Nordpolitik' Part I," *38North*, March 26, 2014, https:// www.38north.org/2014/03/afostercarter032614/.
22. Woong-yong Ha, "Korean Sports in the 1980s and the Seoul Olympic Games of 1988," *Journal of Olympic History* 6, no. 3 (Summer 1998): 11–12.

Chapter 3

1. Data taken from the South Korean Ministry of Unification and tabulated in Oh and Hassig, *North Korea through the Looking Glass* (Washington, DC: Brookings Institution Press, 2000), 44–45.
2. Jonathan Pollack, *No Exit: North Korea, Nuclear Weapons, and International Security* (Abingdon, UK: Routledge, 2011), 101–102.
3. Justin Hastings, *A Most Enterprising Country: North Korea in the Global Economy* (Ithaca, NY: Cornell University Press, 2016), 30.
4. Taik-young Hamm, *Arming the Two Koreas: State, Capital, and Military Power* (London: Routledge, 1999), 86–89.

5. Charles Armstrong, *Tyranny of the Weak: North Korea and the World, 1950–1992* (Ithaca, NY: Cornell University Press, 2015), 252–253.

6. Hakjoon Kim, *Dynasty: The Hereditary Succession Politics of North Korea* (Stanford, CA: Shorenstein Asia-Pacific Research Center, 2017).

7. Marcus Noland, "Famine Deaths, Again," *North Korea Witness to Transformation* (blog), June 30, 2013, https://piie.com/blogs/north-korea-witness-transformation/famine-deaths-again.

8. Sandra Fahy, *Marching through Suffering: Loss and Survival in North Korea* (New York: Columbia University Press, 2015).

9. Hazel Smith, *Hungry for Peace: International Security, Humanitarian Assistance, and Social Change in North Korea* (Washington, DC: United States Institute of Peace, 2005).

10. Stephan Haggard and Marcus Noland, *Hard Target: Sanctions, Inducements, and the Case of North Korea* (Stanford, CA: Stanford University Press, 2017).

Chapter 4

1. "Journal of Soviet Ambassador to the DPRK V. I. Ivanov for 20 January 1956," January 20, 1956, History and Public Policy Program Digital Archive, RGANI Fond 5, Opis 28, Delo 412, Wilson Center Digital Archive, http://digitalarchive.wilsoncenter.org/document/120790. Translated by Gary Goldberg.

2. Dwight D. Eisenhower, "Address to the 470th Plenary Meeting of the United Nations General Assembly," December 8, 1953, International Atomic Energy Association, https://www.iaea.org/about/history/atoms-for-peace-speech.

3. Baya Harrison, "Through the Eyes of the Hermit: The Origins of North Korea's Quest for the Bomb," *Stanford Journal of East Asian Affairs* 7, no. 1 (Winter 2007): 55–59.

4. Richard Nixon, "Informal Remarks in Guam with Newsmen," *The American Presidency Project*, July 25, 1969, http://www.presidency.ucsb.edu/ws/index.php?pid=2140.

5. U.S. Embassy Seoul Cable, "ROK Plans to Develop Nuclear Weapons and Missiles," March 12, 1975, Declassified March 27, 2009, available online via the National Security Archive at https://nsarchive2.gwu.edu//dc.html?doc=3513496-Document-06-U-S-Embassy-Seoul-telegram-8023-to; U.S. Department

of State, "ROK Nuclear Fuel Reprocessing Plans," June 30, 1975, Declassified September 9, 1994, available online via the National Security Archive at https://nsarchive2.gwu.edu//dc.html?doc=3513547-Document-18-State-Department-telegram-195214-to.

6. Mark Fitzpatrick, "Republic of Korea," *Adelphi Series* 55, no. 455 (2016): 18–22.

7. The Wilson Center, *The Carter Chill: US-ROK-DPRK Trilateral Relations, 1976–1979*, A Critical Oral History Conference (Washington, DC: Wilson Center, 2013), https://www.wilsoncenter.org/sites/default/files/NKIDP_The_Carter_Chill_Briefing_Book.pdf; Peter Hayes and Chung-in Moon, "Park Chung Hee, the CIA, and the Bomb," NAPSNet Special Reports, September 23, 2011, https://nautilus.org/napsnet/napsnet-special-reports/park-Chung Hee-the-cia-and-the-bomb/.

8. Director of Central Intelligence, U.S. National Intelligence Estimate, "The Korean Military Balance and Prospects for Hostilities on the Peninsula," NIE 42/14.2-87, March 1987, Declassified June 12, 2010, p. 14, https://www.cia.gov/library/readingroom/docs/DOC_0005569324.pdf.

9. CIA, "Intelligence Assessment of North Korea's Nuclear Efforts," April 28, 1987, U.S. Declassified Documents Online, GALE document number GXONLA309315833; CIA, "Intelligence Special Analysis on Concerns over North Korea's Expansion of Its Nuclear Program, March 22, 1989, U.S. Declassified Documents Online. GALE document number WOBATD108526282.

10. Pollack, *No Exit*, 106.

11. "Joint Declaration of the Denuclearization of the Korean Peninsula," United Nations Peacemaker Database, January 20, 1992, https://peacemaker.un.org/korea-denuclearization92.

12. Mark Manyin and Mary Beth Nitkitin, *Foreign Assistance to North Korea* (Washington, DC: Congressional Research Service Report, 2014), https://fas.org/sgp/crs/row/R40095.pdf.

13. CIA, "Unclassified Report to Congress, July – December 2000," Posted May 2, 2007, https://www.cia.gov/library/reports/archived-reports-1/july_dec2000.htm#5

14. Mike Chinoy, *Meltdown: The Inside Story of the North Korean Nuclear Crisis* (New York: St. Martin's Press, 2008).

15. Condoleezza Rice, *No Higher Honor: A Memoir of My Years in Washington* (New York: Crown, 2011), 158–159.

16. Joint Statement of the Fourth Round of Six Party Talks, September 19, 2005, U.S. Department of State, https://www.state.gov/p/eap/regional/c15455.htm.

17. Japanese Ministry of Foreign Affairs, "Initial Actions for the Implementation of the Joint Statement," February 13, 2007, https://www.mofa.go.jp/region/asia-paci/n_korea/6party/action0702.html.

18. Second-Phase Actions for the Implementation of the September 2005 Joint Statement, October 3, 2007, U.S. Department of State, https://2001-2009.state.gov/r/pa/prs/ps/2007/oct/93217.htm.

19. Peter Crail, "North Korea Delivers Nuclear Declaration," *Arms Control Today*, August 7, 2008, https://www.armscontrol.org/act/2008_07-08/NorthKorea.

20. Peter Crail, "Six Party Talks Stall over Sampling," *Arms Control Today*, January 16, 2009, https://www.armscontrol.org/act/2009_01-02/sixpartytalksstall.

21. Paul Kerr, Steven Hildreth, and Mary Beth Nikitin, *Iran–North Korea–Syria Ballistic Missile and Nuclear Cooperation* (Washington, DC: Congressional Research Service, 2016), https://fas.org/sgp/crs/nuke/R43480.pdf.

22. "Syria's Covert Nuclear Reactor at Al Kibar," YouTube, posted April 25, 2008, https://www.youtube.com/watch?v=4ah6RmcewUM; "Syria's Nuclear Reactor—pt 2," YouTube, posted April 25, 2008, https://www.youtube.com/watch?v=A9HL3NVLZyo.

23. Mike Hayden, "CIA Director Hayden Announces Findings on Covert Syrian Reactor," April 24, 2008, CIA Press Release, https://www.cia.gov/news-information/press-releases-statements/press-release-archive-2008/cia-director-hayden-announces-findings-on-covert-syrian-reactor.html.

24. Michael V. Hayden, "Correcting the Record about that Syrian Nuclear Reactor," *Washington Post*, September 22, 2011.

25. David Sanger and William Broad, "Evidence Is Cited Linking Koreans to Libya Uranium," *New York Times*, May 23, 2004.

26. White House Press Secretary Scott McClellan, "Our Allies Were Not 'Misled,'" Letter to the Editor, *Washington Post*, March 25, 2005, A18.

27. John Haltiwanger, "North Korea 'Handful of Months' from Being Able to Hit U.S. with Nuclear Weapons, CIA Director Warns," *Newsweek*, January 22, 2018.

Chapter 5

1. Japanese Ministry of Foreign Affairs, "Abductions of Japanese Citizens by North Korea," November 6, 2017, https://www. mofa.go.jp/region/asia-paci/n_korea/abduction/index.html.
2. Japanese Ministry of Foreign Affairs, "Statement by the Chief Cabinet Secretary Yohei Kono on the result of the study on the issue of 'comfort women,' " August 4, 1993, https://www.mofa. go.jp/policy/women/fund/state9308.html.

Chapter 6

1. Pew Research Center, Global Indicators Database, accessed August 8, 2018, http://www.pewglobal.org/database/indicator/ 6/country/116/.
2. The United States withdrew its occupation force in 1949, but it retained a US military advisory group in South Korea, which has provided a continuous US military contingent in South Korea since World War II. The token presence in 1949 would increase substantially after North Korea's invasion the following year. "Report by the National Security Council to the President," March 22, 1949, cited in U.S. Department of State, *Foreign Relations of the United States, 1949, The Far East and Australasia,* vol. 7, pt. 2 (Washington, DC: U.S. Government Printing Office, 1976), https:// history.state.gov/historicaldocuments/frus1949v07p2/d209.
3. Clint Work, "The Long History of South Korea's OPCON Debate," *The Diplomat,* November 1, 2017, https://thediplomat. com/2017/11/the-long-history-of-south-koreas-opcon-debate/.
4. Joshua Pollack, "Ballistic Missile Defense in South Korea: Separate Systems against a Common Threat," CISSM (Center for International and Security Studies at Maryland) Collection of Papers, January 2017, http://www.cissm.umd.edu/ sites/default/files/Paper%204%20-%20Ballistic%20Missile%20 Defense%20in%20South%20Korea.pdf.
5. Center for Strategic and International Studies (CSIS), "South Korea Suspends THAAD Deployment," CSIS Missile Defense Project, June 7, 2017, https://missilethreat.csis.org/south-korea-suspends-thaad-deployment/.
6. Edward Alden and Scott Snyder, "Why U.S.-Korea Trade Deal Matters," Council on Foreign Relations Expert Brief, December 6, 2010, https://www.cfr.org/expert-brief/ why-us-korea-trade-deal-matters.

7. Patrick Gillepsie, "New US Deal with South Korea: What You Need to Know," *CNN Money*, March 28, 2018, https://money.cnn.com/2018/03/27/news/economy/us-south-korea-trade-deal/index.html.

Chapter 7

1. Norimitsu Onishi, "South Korea's President Sags in Opinion Polls," *New York Times*, November 27, 2006, A6.

Chapter 8

1. Leonid Petrov, "The Politics of Inter-Korean Economic Cooperation: 1998–2009," *Asia-Pacific Journal*, vol. 7, issue 29, no. 3 (July 20, 2009), https://apjjf.org/-Leonid-Petrov/3190/article.html.
2. Roger Cavazos, "Mind the Gap between Rhetoric and Reality," NAPSNet Special Reports, June 26, 2012, https://nautilus.org/napsnet/napsnet-special-reports/mind-the-gap-between-rhetoric-and-reality/.
3. Motoko Rich, "In North Korea, 'Surgical Strike Could Spin into 'Worst Kind of Fighting,'" *New York Times*, July 5, 2017, A1.
4. The Joint Civilian-Military Investigation Group, "Investigation Result on the Sinking of the ROKS 'Cheonan,'" May 20, 2010, http://news.bbc.co.uk/nol/shared/bsp/hi/pdfs/20_05_10jigreport.pdf.
5. David Cyranoski, "Controversy over South Korea's Sunken Ship," *Nature*, July 14, 2010, https://www.nature.com/news/2010/100708/full/news.2010.343.html.
6. Song Sang-ho, "N.K. Artillery Strikes S.K. Island," *Korea Herald*, November 23, 2010.

Chapter 9

1. Patrick McEachern and Jaclyn O'Brien McEachern, *North Korea, Iran, and the Challenge to International Order* (New York: Routledge, 2017), 67.
2. Stephan Haggard and Marcus Noland, *Hard Target: Sanctions, Inducements, and the Case of North Korea* (Stanford, CA: Stanford University Press, 2017).
3. World Bank, "Trade Summary for Korea, Rep. 2016," accessed July 9, 2018, https://wits.worldbank.org/countrysnapshot/en/KOR.

4. Chen Kane and Miles A. Pomper, "Reactor Race: South Korea's Nuclear Export Successes and Challenges," KEIA (Korea Economic Institute of America) Academic Paper Series, May 21, 2013, http://www.keia.org/sites/default/files/publications/south_koreas_nuclear_export_successes_and_challenges.pdf.

5. Korea Customs Service, "Import/Export by Country," accessed July 31, 2018, http://www.customs.go.kr/kcshome/trade/TradeCountryList.do.

6. UN Security Council, "Report of the Panel of Experts Established Pursuant to Resolution 1874 (2009)," March 5, 2018, http://www.un.org/ga/search/view_doc.asp?symbol=S/2018/171.

7. DPRK Ministry of Foreign Affairs, "DPRK Terms U.S. Hostile Policy Main Obstacle in Resolving Nuclear Issue," Korean Central News Agency (KCNA), August 31, 2012.

8. Andray Abrahamian and Curtis Melvin, "North Korea's Special Economic Zones: Plans vs. Progress," 38North Special Report, November 23, 2015, https://www.38north.org/wp-content/uploads/pdf/2015-11-23_North-Koreas-SEZ-Plans-vs-Progress.pdf.

Chapter 10

1. For more on the Songbun system, see Robert Collins, *Marked for Life: Songbun, North Korea's Social Classification System* (Washington, DC: Committee for Human Rights in North Korea, 2012), https://www.hrnk.org/uploads/pdfs/HRNK_Songbun_Web.pdf.

2. Stephan Haggard and Marcus Noland, *Witness to Transformation: Refugee Insights into North Korea* (Washington, DC: Peterson Institute for International Economics, 2011), 75–77.

3. Nat Kretchun, Catherine Lee, and Seamus Tuohy, "Compromising Connectivity: Information Dynamics between the State and Society in a Digitizing North Korea," Intermedia, 2017, http://www.intermedia.org/wp-content/uploads/2017/02/Compromising-Connectivity-Final-Report_Soft-Copy.pdf.

4. Timothy Martin and Warangkana Chomchuen, "North Korea Gets Smartphones, and the Regime Keeps Tabs," *Wall Street Journal*, December 6, 2017.

5. For more detail on North Korea's cell phones, see Yonho Kim, *Cell Phones in North Korea: Has North Korea Entered the Telecommunications Revolution?* (Washington, DC: US Korea Institute at SAIS (School of Advanced International Studies)

and Voice of America, 2014), https://38north.org/wp-content/uploads/2014/03/Kim-Yonho-Cell-Phones-in-North-Korea.pdf.

6. Global Security, "Korea-Regionalism," November 13, 2016, https://www.globalsecurity.org/military/world/rok/regionalism.htm.

7. Korean Culture and Information Service, Ministry of Culture, Sports, and Tourism, "Hallyu (Korean Wave)," accessed August 1, 2018, http://www.korea.net/AboutKorea/Culture-and-the-Arts/Hallyu.

8. Organisation for Economic Co-operation and Development, *Education at a Glance 2017: OECD Indicators* (Paris: OECD, 2017), 51, https://www.oecd-ilibrary.org/docserver/eag-2017-en.pdf?expires=1530795542&id=id&accname=guest&checksum=2F19D63BE77AB31ECCBF6CCA7C788F4C.

9. Organisation for Economic Co-operation and Development, "Suicide Rates," 2018, OECD Data, accessed August 10, 2018, https://data.oecd.org/healthstat/suicide-rates.htm.

Chapter 11

1. United Nations, "Universal Declaration of Human Rights," December 10, 1948, http://www.un.org/en/universal-declaration-human-rights/index.html.

2. UN Office of the High Commissioner for Human Rights, "Situation of Human Rights in the Democratic People's Republic of Korea," April 16, 2003, http://ap.ohchr.org/documents/alldocs.aspx?doc_id=4960.

3. UN Human Rights Council, "Report on the Commission of Inquiry on Human Rights in the Democratic People's Republic of Korea," February 7, 2014, https://www.ohchr.org/EN/HRBodies/HRC/CoIDPRK/Pages/ReportoftheCommissionofInquiryDPRK.aspx.

4. Blaine Harden, *Escape from Camp 14* (New York: Penguin, 2013). The defector's account changed in some respects, which led North Korea to criticize it as a complete fabrication. Defector accounts, compounded by trauma, often mistake certain details, including significant ones, and this account appeared to be no different. The cited 2013 reprint edition corrects these errors.

5. Prevalence of stunting among five-year-old children in North Korea in 2015 was 27.9 percent. The Asia Pacific average was 29.5 percent. See Food and Agriculture Organization, *Regional*

Overview of Food Security and Nutrition Asia and the Pacific
(Rome: Food and Agriculture Organization, 2017), 10, http://
www.fao.org/3/i7930en/I7930EN.pdf.

6. For simplified access to North Korean trade data, see "Total
Import Data," East-West Center and National Committee on
North Korea, North Korea in the World, accessed September
30, 2018, https://www.northkoreaintheworld.org/economic/
import-breakdown.

FURTHER READING

Books

Armstrong, Charles. *Tyranny of the Weak: North Korea and the World, 1950–1992*. Ithaca, NY: Cornell University Press, 2015.

Cha, Victor. *Powerplay: The Origins of the American Alliance System in Asia*. Princeton, NJ: Princeton University Press, 2016.

Fahy, Sandra. *Dying for Rights: Putting North Korea's Human Rights Abuses on the Record*. New York: Columbia University Press, 2019.

Glosserman, Brad, and Scott Snyder. *The Japan–South Korea Identity Clash: East Asian Security and the United States*. New York: Columbia University Press, 2015.

Haggard, Stephan, and Marcus Noland. *Hard Target: Sanctions, Inducements, and the Case of North Korea*. Stanford, CA: Stanford University Press, 2017.

Hastings, Justin. *A Most Enterprising Country: North Korea in the Global Economy*. Ithaca, NY: Cornell University Press, 2016.

Kim, Hakjoon. *Dynasty: The Hereditary Succession Politics of North Korea*. Stanford, CA: Shorenstein Asia-Pacific Research Center, 2017.

Lankov, Andrei. *The Real North Korea: Life and Politics in the Failed Stalinist Utopia*. New York: Oxford University Press, 2014.

McEachern, Patrick, and Jaclyn O'Brien McEachern. *North Korea, Iran, and the Challenge to International Order*. New York: Routledge, 2017.

Oberdorfer, Don, and Robert Carlin. *The Two Koreas: A Contemporary History*. Rev. ed. New York: Basic Books, 2013.

Pollack, Jonathan. *No Exit: North Korea, Nuclear Weapons, and International Security*. Abingdon: Routledge, 2011.

Smith, Hazel. *North Korea: Markets and Military Rule.* Cambridge, UK: Cambridge University Press, 2015.

Snyder, Scott. *South Korea at the Crossroads: Autonomy and Alliance in an Era of Rival Powers.* New York: Columbia University Press, 2018.

Stueck, William. *The Korean War: An International History.* Princeton, NJ: Princeton University Press, 1995.

English-language online resources

38North.org. A webpage dedicated to scholarly analysis of North Korea with a focus on current events.

Arms Control Association (ACA). https://www.armscontrol.org/country/9/date. ACA provides useful chronologies and assessments of North Korea's nuclear and missile activity.

Central Intelligence Agency (CIA). *The World Factbook.* https://www.cia.gov/library/publications/the-world-factbook/.

Congressional Research Service (CRS) reports. CRS has produced multiple timely and well-researched unclassified reports on North Korea. Though the CRS has not made these reports public directly, they can be found on several webpages, including the Federation of American Scientists, https://fas.org/sgp/crs/index.html. Since this site's search function is limited, researchers will be best served using a general Internet search that includes "CRS report" and the specific topic of interest.

East-West Center and National Committee on North Korea. "North Korea in the World." https://www.northkoreaintheworld.org/. This webpage provides easily accessible data on North Korea's external relations.

South Korean government data. The South Korean government collects and presents in English some of its data on North Korea. South Korea's Ministry of Unification provides data on inter-Korean cooperation and exchanges. http://www.unikorea.go.kr/eng_unikorea/relations/statistics/traffic/. A webpage dedicated to the 2018 inter-Korean summit provides the latest official South Korean view on inter-Korean affairs. http://www.korea.net/Government/Current-Affairs/National-Affairs?affairId=656. South Korea's central bank, the Bank of Korea, publishes annual estimates of North Korea's economy, but its site is difficult to search in English. A better source for North Korean economic news is *NK Econ Watch* (blog). http://www.nkeconwatch.com/.

South Korean newspapers. The three highest circulation South Korean
  newspapers have English language sites. These are Chosun Ilbo
  http://english.chosun.com/, Donga Ilbo http://english.donga.
  com/, and Joongang Ilbo http://koreajoongangdaily.joins.com/.
  These three newspapers lean conservative politically, the most
  significant progressive-leaning South Korean newspaper is
  Hankyoreh. http://english.hani.co.kr/. American newspapers with
  significant coverage of Korean issues include the *New York Times*,
  the *Washington Post*, and the *Wall Street Journal*.
Wilson Center Digital Archive. Modern Korean History Portal. http://
  digitalarchive.wilsoncenter.org/theme/modern-korean-history-
  portal. This resource provides easy access to many primary
  documents related to Korea, translated into English.

INDEX